How to Involve Children
in
Worship Services

How to Involve Children in Worship Services

by
James H. and R. Darline Robinson

Concordia
Publishing House
St. Louis

Concordia Publishing House, St. Louis, Missouri
Copyright © 1980, Concordia Publishing House

Printed in the United States of America

Library of Congress Cataloging in Publication Data

Robinson, James H. 1930—
    How to involve children in worship
service.

    1. Children's liturgies. I. Robinson,
Rowena D., joint author. II. Title.
BV199.C4R62   264   80-13159
ISBN 0-570-03807-3

Dedicated to our mothers:
Mrs. Amanda Honig
Mrs. Sophia Robinson

and in memory of our fathers:
John W. Robinson
Roland C. Honig

Contents

Foreword

Young Christians are an important part of God's kingdom and of the church. Noticing that in most congregations children are not often involved in the worship services, other than singing a song or participating in a Christmas service, has prompted us to share these children's worship ideas. We believe that children are included when the Bible reminds us to worship, praise, and rejoice in our Lord. Too often, the worship service must be geared to an adult level. Here are 24 ways to include young Christians in a special way in the regular worship service.

If you involve your young Christians in worship services, as suggested in this book, you will observe some pleasant things happening. Church attendance will increase because parents love to see their children involved in the service. Many parents who have not been in church for a while will attend when their children are participating. The Holy Spirit can renew that spark of faith in their hearts to attend more often. Attendance in your midweek and Sunday school classes will also increase, because children must be present at one of these to practice for the worship service. Best of all, you will notice an eagerness and joy in the children as they feel a part of the worship services also. It gives them an opportunity to publicly witness their faith.

An additional feature of this book is that the services are ready to use or easily adapted. Your leader will not have to spend a lot of time planning the children's participation. Time of the year, music, including the processionals and recessionals; children's speaking parts; and the visual ideas, such as banners and posters, are all suggested in this book. A minimum of rehearsal time is needed. Songs can be practiced in weekday school, Sunday school openings, or in the Christian day school music period, giving children a good motivation for practice. Speaking parts are not to be memorized but read by the children, after first practicing with teacher guidance. One rehearsal with all the children present is necessary, preferably the Saturday morning before the service.

All the services in this book can be inserted into the regular morning worship service. The children's participation is intended to be a part of the service, and does not have to be a special service, although if desired, many of these could. The processionals and recessionals that are suggested help to enhance the service. The children's choir selections have been chosen with care and can be placed in the part of the service where the regular choir would normally sing. The speaking parts are usually brief and can be placed in the liturgical setting, perhaps somewhere under the ministry of the Word, sometimes as a reading of the lesson for the day. The visuals are important, because they set the theme or mood of the service. In most cases you can involve your children in making these.

To get the best involvement of children in these services your director of Christian education, school principal, music director, teacher, or leader should keep a record of the children involved in speaking parts, in making visuals, and in special singing groups of a particular service. In this way you will know to use other children for the next service, thus involving all of them through the year. Parents will be pleased to know that their children will have a speaking part at some time during the year. Many times children are unable to be present for the children's Christmas service. These children should be included, so that all will have had an opportunity to participate through the year. We believe that children should not be started too young as speaking participants, because this could begin fears that could affect their later church life. Perhaps the very young should be included only in the singing part of the service, and the speaking parts should be reserved for those who can read.

The Visuals: Suggestions for visuals include banners, posters, tagboard banners, write-on slides, display boards, flags, word and letter cards. Theater posters, 28"x44", and regular posters, 22"x28", are suggested for use. All banner designs can also be used on the theater posters. Posters are mounted on poles in various arrangements. We urge you to involve as many children as possible in the making of the visuals. Supervised work is neat work that will enhance the service. You may want to consider one of the ladies' circles to assist in making the cloth banners.

For all the visuals there are suggestions for size, color, or materials. For many of the banners, posters, and flags transparencies can be made of the designs in this book. By projecting your transparency on the wall you can have any size suitable to your needs. If your church or school does not have an overhead projector, one may be borrowed from the public school or elsewhere. You will find that the children will enjoy working on difficult visuals, such as tagboard banners. Make certain that your letters are large enough to be clearly seen from the last pew in the church.

All of the visuals are an important part of the service. In some of the services the visuals emphasize the theme of the service, other visuals are correlated with music selections, still others are used with The Spoken Word.

We suggest that you keep all patterns for each design on file. This will save you time for later performances. You will also be able to make new visuals by regrouping the cutouts and letters. You will also find that your school and church can use these visuals in other ways, such as displays in Sunday school departments or in classrooms. Many of these made in miniature form could make craft items for art classes and vacation Bible schools.

Number of Copies Needed: In order to effectively use these materials it is recommended that enough copies be purchased for the various leaders. Your DCE or principal will need his copy. The pastor, organist, visuals person, and teachers involved should have a copy. Children need not have a copy; however, enough copies for children with speaking parts will save time and duplicating cost.

Acknowledgments

Children's script for Chapter 7 is taken from the *Bible Story Book* by Elsie E. Egermeier, Concordia Publishing House, 1922.

Script for Chapters 1, 2, 10, 11, 12, 15, and 24 is from the *Concordia Bible Story Book* by Arthur W. Gross, © 1971, Concordia Publishing House. Used by permission.

Script for Chapters 9, 16 (part), 22, and 23 and other references marked TEV are used by permission of American Bible Society, from the *Good News Bible*, copyright © TEV, 1966, 1971, 1976.

Isolated passages in Chapters 14 and 17 marked KJV are from the King James Version.

Script for Chapter 14 and all other Scripture references are from the Revised Standard Version of the Bible, copyright 1946, 1952, © 1971, 1973 by the Division of Christian Education of the National Council of the Churches of Christ in the U.S.A., and used by permission.

"The Magnificat with Motions for Pantomime Choir," Chapter 24, is from the children's Christmas service "Christ Is Born Today," Concordia Publishing House, 1968.

Preparing the Children
for the Service

Services are offered for appropriate times during the church year. There are 24 services in this book. We have found that using about six each year is effective, but your local circumstances will suggest the frequency with which the services are used.

Theme of Service: Services are prepared to correspond to the seasons or festivals of the church year.

Children's Participation: This section contains the elements and/or procedures for the children's participation.

Processionals and Recessionals: Most of the hymns chosen can be found in both *The Lutheran Hymnal* (TLH) and the *Service Book and Hymnal* (SBH). Many of the titles can be found also in other hymnals.

The Choirs: To obtain the best involvement of children we have suggested songs for youngsters and older children. One of the songs should be sung in the regular place in the service designated for the choir. At times a song will be sung as part of The Spoken Word section. The other(s) are up to the discretion of the pastor or leader. The selection of children's songs has been taken largely from the following list:
Children Sing Series, Fortress Press
The Children's Hymnal (TCH), Concordia Publishing House
A Child's Garden of Song, Concordia Publishing House
Folk Encounter, Hope Publishing Co.
Folk Hymnal for the Now Generation, Singspiration
Hymns Hot and Carols Cool, Proclamation Productions, Inc.
Joyful Sounds, Concordia Publishing House
The Little Christian's Songbook, Concordia Publishing House
A New Now, Hope Publishing Co.
Primaries Sing, Scripture Press
Sing for Joy, Seabury Press
Sing to the Lord, Scripture Press
Young Children Sing, Augsburg Publishing House
Some of the songs may be found also in songbooks other than those listed in the chapters.

The Spoken Word: Children will be involved in reading a particular Bible story, reading a psalm responsively, teaching by acrostics, reading about the work of a hero of faith such as Martin Luther, reading the narrative for slides, or reading selected Bible verses. Bible stories, excerpted from the *Concordia Bible Story Book* or *Egermeier's Bible Story Book,* are broken into individual speaking parts. All of the speaking parts are printed in this book.

Care must be taken to work with the children in practicing their speaking parts well. The congregation will soon be discouraged if the children cannot read well and do not enunciate clearly. We suggest using a microphone so that all in the church can hear the children speak. Some speaking parts are larger than others, and should be assigned to those children who speak well. We suggest a speaker's stand be placed up front to one side, and the speaking parts placed on it. Then children will not be holding papers in their hands. Children should line up in the order in which they speak and read their parts from the page on the stand. The microphone should also be placed at the stand. Individual parts for the children may be duplicated for study and rehearsal.

1. The Wise Men Worship Jesus

Children's Participation

Processional Hymn: "Brightest and Best of the Sons of the Morning," TLH, SBH (congregation). The poster bearer will lead pastor(s), children, and teachers into the house of worship.

Poster: They Came from the East

The Choirs: "What Star Is This," *Joyful Sounds* (older children)
"Many Years Ago," *Primaries Sing* (younger children)

The Spoken Word: The children read the account of "The Wise Men from the East" taken from the *Concordia Bible Story Book* (between the Scripture readings or in place of the Gospel lesson).

1. Some time after Jesus was born and while Mary and Joseph were still in Bethlehem, a surprising thing happened. From a country far to the east, probably Babylon, some wise men called Magi came to Jerusalem. These men studied the stars.

2. One night back home they had seen a special star in the sky. Somehow they had come to know a prophecy which said that a King would be born in the land of Judah, who would be the Savior of all people.

3. The Wise Men believed that the strange star was the sign that the prophecy had been fulfilled. So firmly did the Wise Men believe this that they started out at once to find the newborn King. They wanted to see Him with their own eyes and honor Him. In their baggage they carried precious gifts for the new King.

4. Riding on camels, the Wise Men traveled hundreds of weary miles, making their way across hot deserts, along dangerous mountain paths, and through deep valleys until they finally reached Jerusalem, the capital city of Judah. There they hoped to get some information about the newborn King.

5. Supposing that nearly everyone would know something about Him, they stopped some passersby and said, "Where is the Child who is to be King of the Jews? We have seen His star in the eastern skies and have come to worship Him."

6. The people of Jerusalem looked curiously at the strangers. Although they lived only six miles from Bethlehem, they did not know that the Christ Child, their Savior and King, had been born. They could not give the Wise Men the information they wanted.

7. But some suspicious person thought that King Herod, who ruled in Jerusalem at the time, should know that certain strangers were in the city looking for a new king. Herod became greatly upset when he heard this. He had been a cruel king, and he feared that the people might take sides with the new King and force him off the throne.

8. The people of Jerusalem were also upset. They knew that the baby King would have many followers, for he was a descendant of David, their beloved king. They also knew that if the followers would try to put the new King on the throne, Herod would call out his army, and then there would be bloody fighting in the streets.

9. It seemed to Herod that an emergency had arisen and that something had to be done at once. He called a meeting of the chief priests and scribes and

asked them where the Messiah was to be born. The answer was easy, for the priests and scribes knew the Old Testament prophecies well.

10. "The new King is to be born in Bethlehem of Judah," they said. "For it is written, 'And you Bethlehem in the land of Judah are by no means the least among the leading towns of Judah; for from you there shall come a leader who will be the Ruler of My people Israel.' "

11. Herod believed the prophecy and decided to do away with the baby King as quickly as possible. He sent for the Wise Men and held a secret meeting with them.

12. Supposing the new star had appeared exactly when the new King was born, Herod had the Wise Men tell him when they had first seen the star. For if he knew this, he could easily tell about how old baby Jesus must be. And then he would know how big a child he would have to look for.

13. When Herod had the information he wanted, he sent the Wise Men on to Bethlehem, saying, "Go and search carefully for the little Child. When you have found Him, come back and tell me where He is, so I too may go and bow down before Him." Actually Herod meant to kill Jesus.

14. It was night when the Wise Men left Herod's palace. As they looked up, they had a delightful surprise. There was the star again—the same star they had seen in the East! Now it was moving south, and the Wise Men followed it.

15. The star kept leading them until it came to Bethlehem. There it stopped where Mary and Joseph were staying. When the Wise Men went inside, they found Mary and baby Jesus.

16. At once they humbly knelt down and worshiped Him. Then they opened their treasure chests and presented Jesus with precious gifts—gold and two kinds of sweet-smelling perfume called frankincense and myrrh.

17. Now the Wise Men were ready to return home. Since they did not know about Herod's plan to kill the Christ Child, they probably meant to go by way of Jerusalem, so they might tell Herod where to find the new King.

18. But God appeared to them in a dream and told them not to return to Herod. The Wise Men obeyed God. Instead of taking a road that led through Jerusalem, they returned to their home in the East by another way.

Recessional: "Hail to the Lord's Annointed" TLH, SBH (congregation). Poster bearer, pastor(s), children, and teachers leave the sanctuary during the singing of this hymn.

Materials needed

1. three poster boards, 22"x28", such as light blue, light green, or brown
2. black or white construction paper for letters
3. assorted colors of construction paper to make colorful cutouts

Note: Assorted metallic papers work well for this kind of poster. Try a white or a cream-colored background. You may want to make this design as a banner, using silhouettes, sequins, etc.

2. The Twelve-Year-Old Jesus in the Temple

Children's Participation

Processional Hymn: "Let Us Ever Walk with Jesus," TLH (congregation). Two poster bearers lead the pastor(s), children, and teachers into the sanctuary.

Posters: Walk in the Way of the Lord and Learn like the Boy Jesus

The Choirs: "We Are in God's House Today," TCH, *A Child's Garden of Song* (younger children)
"When We Walk with the Lord," *Joyful Sounds* (older children)
"Abide, O Dearest Jesus," sts. 1—3, TLH, TCH, *Joyful Sounds* (older children)

The Spoken Word: (between the Scripture readings) The children will read the account of Jesus in the temple, in the words taken from the *Concordia Bible Story Book.*

1. During His boyhood years Jesus lived with Mary and Joseph in the village of Nazareth. There He also grew to manhood. Because Joseph was a woodworker, the people of Nazareth came to speak of Jesus as "Joseph the Carpenter's son."

2. The Bible tells us very little about Jesus' boyhood years, but we may be sure that in many ways He lived like the other boys of His age—that He played with the children in the neighborhood, helped Joseph in the carpenter shop, ran errands for His mother, went to school, and worshiped in the synagog.

3. But in one way Jesus was different from everyone else. Since He was the Son of God as well as a human being, He had no sin. He was born without sin, and in His whole life He never thought or said or did anything that was evil, but always did what was good and pleasing to His Father in heaven.

4. As time passed, Jesus must have noticed that every year in the springtime the Jewish people of Nazareth went to Jerusalem to celebrate a great church festival called the feast of the Passover. Mary and Joseph always went along. But up to the time when Jesus was 12 years old, He had to stay home, for the rules of the Jewish people did not allow boys under the age of 12 to take part in the Passover celebrations.

5. One can easily imagine how happy Jesus must have been when He could go along to Jerusalem, about 70 miles away, and worship His heavenly Father in the beautiful temple there.

6. The people who were going to make the trip to the Passover feast assembled on the main road and traveled as a company. As they passed through cities and villages, more and more people joined them. Thus the procession became quite large. But this was not the only procession making its way to Jerusalem. Others were coming from all directions.

7. The people walked or rode on camels and donkeys. When mealtime came, they sat down by the side of the road and ate the food they had brought with them. When nighttime came, they went into the nearby fields and lay down on mats or rugs around a campfire and slept under the starry sky.

8. How happy they were when they reached Jerusalem! For seven days

they celebrated the feast of the Passover. They recalled how hundreds of years before the Lord freed their ancestors from slavery in Egypt.

9. They also recalled how the Lord spared the firstborn sons of their ancestors by having the death angel pass over their houses while going through the land and killing the firstborn son in every Egyptian family. They thanked and praised God for His merciful goodness.

10. After the feast the people of Nazareth and the people from other places started on their way home. But Jesus stayed behind in Jerusalem. Mary and Joseph did not know this. They thought He was somewhere in the crowd going their way.

11. But when Mary and Joseph had traveled a whole day without seeing Jesus, they became worried and began to look for Him. They went through the entire company of their friends and relatives and asked again and again whether anyone had seen Jesus. But each time they received the disappointing answer, "No we have not seen Him."

12. Then Mary and Joseph went all the way back to Jerusalem. They inquired about Jesus in every place they thought He might be. No one had seen Him. Finally, on the third day of their search Mary and Joseph looked in the temple.

13. There was Jesus! He was sitting in the midst of a group of well-educated teachers, talking with them about things of the Bible. Jesus listened to the teachers and asked or answered questions.

14. All the teachers were amazed, for Jesus had an understanding of God and of the Scriptures far beyond what they had seen in other children.

15. Mary and Joseph were also amazed—at seeing Jesus among those learned men. What Jesus was doing was good, but Mary could not quickly forget how worried she and Joseph had been. She said to Jesus, "Son why have You done this? Anxiously Your father and I have been looking for You."

16. Then Jesus said to Mary, "What made you search for Me? Don't you know that I must be in My Father's house?" He meant to remind Mary that He was the Son of God and that He was getting ready to do the work for which His heavenly Father sent Him.

17. Mary kept His words in her heart and thought about them many times. She was sure that the heavenly Father had sent Jesus for some great purpose.

18. Jesus returned to Nazareth with His parents and was obedient to them. As the days and weeks passed, Jesus grew bigger and stronger. He also grew in His understanding of the Scriptures. The people who knew Him loved Him, and His heavenly Father loved Him too.

Recessional: "O Savior, Precious Savior," TLH, SBH (congregation). Poster bearers, pastor(s), children, and teachers leave the sanctuary during this hymn.

Materials needed

1. black poster boards, 22"x28"
2. white construction paper for church, Bible, and lamp
3. bright green trees
4. yellow-orange, orange, gold, red-orange for letters, using the brightest color for the words "Learn like the boy Jesus"—add light aqua words if you like

3. Jesus for All Nations

Children's Participation

Processional Hymn: "Jesus Shall Reign Where'er the Sun," TLH, SBH (congregation). During the singing of this hymn, pastor(s), children, and teachers process into the sanctuary. Children in the acrostic carry their letter cards in with them.

The Choirs: "Jesus Loves the Little Children," *Primaries Sing* (younger children)
"Arise, O God, and Shine," TLH, TCH (older children)

The Spoken Word: "Jesus for All Nations" A Children's Acrostic which tells about important mission work carried on by our church will be utilized by younger children. If the children cannot memorize the speaking parts, you may wish to type each child's speaking part on paper and tape or glue it to the back of the letter cards for the children to read. Each child places his letter on the display board before he speaks. If you do not wish to use a display board, make larger letter cards. Have the children line up in front of the church and hold up their letter card as they speak.

1. *J* Jesus died for all people. He said, "Go and teach all nations, baptizing them in the name of the Father, and of the Son, and of the Holy Spirit."
2. *E* Everyone needs to know what Jesus has done for them. He loves them very much, and wants them in His kingdom.
3. *S* Several different workers are needed in our mission fields such as pastors, teachers, doctors, and nurses.
4. *U* Until we send more workers, there will be people who never hear that Jesus loves them and saved them from their sins.
5. *S* Sending missionaries to other countries is important work of the church.

6. *F* For years, children have been learning about mission work in other countries. Some become missionaries when they have finished their schooling.
7. *O* Other children help by praying for our missionaries, asking God to bless their work, to give them healthy bodies so they are able to continue their work for us.
8. *R* Regular offerings given in our church schools are sent to the missionaries so they can buy needed equipment and materials in their work.

9. *A* All Christians should be anxious to share the Good News—which is God's love for all.
10. *L* Little children, school children, teenagers, and adults can all help in this work.
11. *L* Let's all work to help our fellow Christians in other countries share the love of Jesus with those who know so little about Him.

12. *N* National missionaries must be trained so they can work in their own countries.
13. *A* Additional money is needed for colleges and seminaries to train these nationals.

14. *T* Traditions and cultures of these nationals must also be studied by our missionaries who are sent to be instructors in these schools.
15. *I* Instructors for those colleges and seminaries need special education and training in the languages they will be using.
16. *O* Other workers are needed to study foreign languages so that materials can be written for missionaries and instructors to use in their important work.
17. *N* National pastors and teachers can be very effective in the new churches started in these countries.
18. *S* Souls can be won for Jesus in every part of the world through the mission work of our church. We must always carry out the command of our Savior when He said, "Teach all nations . . . and remember, I am with you always."

The Offering: A large box decorated in red and white with the words "Hearts for Jesus" is placed at the front of the altar. The children file to the box and place their offerings in it. Their offerings can be taped to a red heart that has been given them the week before.

After the other offerings have been received by the pastor, children pray one of the following offering prayers:

> Our hands we fold, our heads we bow,
> Our gifts, dear God, we give you now. Amen

> We give Thee but Thine own, Whate'er the gift may be;
> All that we have is Thine alone, A trust, O Lord, from Thee. (TLH, SBH)

Recessional Hymn: "Hark the Voice of Jesus Crying," TLH, SBH. Pastor(s), children and teachers leave the sanctuary during this hymn.

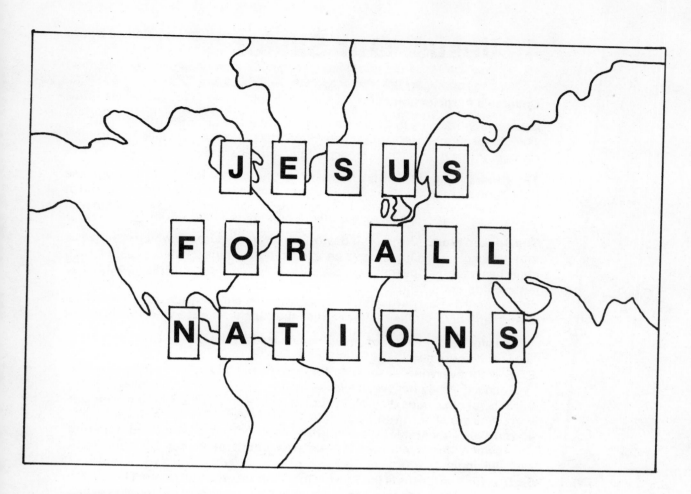

Materials needed

1. one display board, at least 3'x4'
2. large world map for background, about 3'x4'
3. construction paper for 18 letter cards, each 4"x6"
4. 3" letter patterns

4. Jesus, Our Savior

Children's Participation

Processional: "Come to Calvary's Holy Mountain," TLH, SBH (congregation). The pastor(s), children, and teachers process into the sanctuary during the singing of this hymn. Children carry their letter cards with them.

The Choirs: "Let Me Learn of Jesus," *A Child's Garden of Song* (younger children)

"Glory Be to Jesus" *Joyful Sounds* (older children)

The Spoken Word: "Jesus, Our Savior," a children's acrostic which reminds us that Jesus gave His life to save people from their sins, is utilized. After each child has said his speech, he places the letter card on a display board. The letter cards are arranged in the form of a cross. If you do not wish to use a display board, make larger letter cards. Have the children line up in front of the church and hold up their letter card as they speak.

1. *J* is for the first letter of Jesus' name. Jesus is the Son of God, my Savior and yours also.
2. *E* is for everyone. Jesus died for the sins of all people. Everyone can be saved if they believe in Him as Savior.
3. *S* is for sin. Jesus died on the cross for the sins of the whole world. Our sins are all forgiven.
4. *U* is for unbearable. We would say that the punishment and suffering which Jesus endured for us was unbearable. Yet He suffered it willingly.
5. *S* is for Son. Jesus is the Son of God. God showed the greatest love when He had His Son take the punishment for the sins of all people.
6. *O* is for only. Only Jesus, the Son of God, can save us and give us heaven. Do you believe in Him as your personal Savior? I do.
7. *U* is for upon. It was upon a cross that Jesus, our Savior died for the sins of the whole world.
8. *R* is for Redeemer. We can call Jesus our Redeemer. He is our great Redeemer, whom we love.
9. *S* is for satisfied. God was satisfied with the suffering and death of Jesus.
10. *A* is for all. Jesus paid the price which takes away all sins. How happy we should be that our sins are all forgiven.
11. *V* is for very. During Lent we are very sad that Jesus had to die for our sins. But we are very happy that He willingly did it and that He rose again.
12. *I* is for I'll. I'll thank Jesus every day for giving me the promise of heaven. I'll serve Him all my days.
13. *O* is for on. It was on Good Friday that Jesus our Savior died on the cross. It was on Easter that He rose from the dead.
14. *R* is for realize. Do you realize what Jesus has done for you? Many people do not fully appreciate what a great sacrifice He made for us. I hope all of you realize that He is your Savior.

Recessional Hymn: "I Lay My Sins on Jesus," TLH, SBH (congregation). Pastor(s), teachers, and children leave the sanctuary during this hymn.

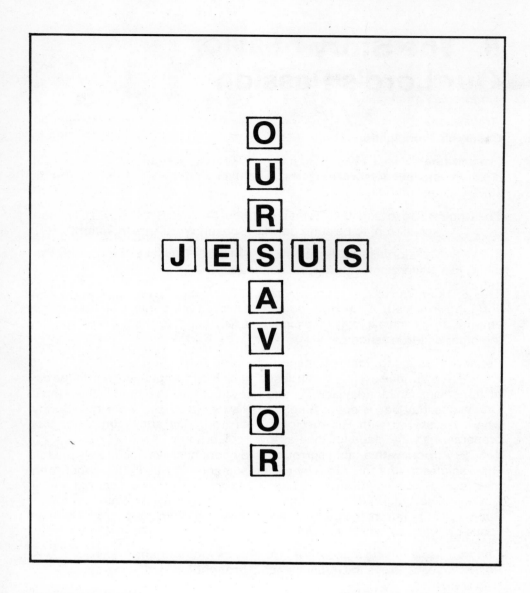

Materials needed

1. one display board, 3'x4'; background, gold, lavender, grey, or red
2. black construction paper for letter cards, 4"x4"
3. white construction paper and 2" letter patterns

Note: White symbols of the Passion story mounted on black construction paper could also be added to the display board. Make 4 of them to add one in each corner.

5. The Story of Our Lord's Passion

Children's Participation

Processional: "Jesus, I Will Ponder Now," TLH (congregation). The pastor(s), children, and teachers will enter the sanctuary. Four children will carry in the small posters.

The Choirs: "Go to Dark Gethsemane," *Joyful Sounds,* SBH, TLH, TCH (older children, to be sung during "Spoken Word" presentation)

"Glory Be to Jesus," TLH, SBH, TCH (all children during the silent prayer, after the benediction)

The Spoken Word: Children will recount the main events of our Lord's suffering and death. At the time indicated children will display Lenten symbols emphasizing each event as they explain it. Stanzas 1, 2, and 3 will be sung by the older children as indicated.

Begin by displaying *Poster 1:* Institution of the Lord's Supper

1. On Sunday of Holy Week Jesus made His triumphal entry into the city of Jerusalem. On Monday and Tuesday He spent time teaching in the temple. On Wednesday Jesus spent time with His disciples and went to Bethany, where He stayed with His disciples until Thursday afternoon. After this, preparations were made for the Passover celebration.

2. A room with a table surrounded by couches was needed. Jesus told His disciples to find this room by asking someone. It was in this upper room that Jesus Himself instituted the Lord's Supper. He told His disciples and all Christians to celebrate this Supper often. When we celebrate the Lord's Supper in our church, the pastors repeat the words of institution which Jesus spoke on this first Maundy Thursday.

Children rise and sing stanza 1 of "Go to Dark Gethsemane."
Poster 2: Jesus Prays in Gethsemane, is brought forward while the children sing stanza 1.

3. After singing a hymn Jesus and His disciples left the upper room and walked slowly to the Mount of Olives. At the foot of this mount Jesus entered the Garden of Gethsemane with Peter, James, and John. Jesus knew what lay ahead and felt the need to pray earnestly to His heavenly Father.

4. Jesus gave us a good example to follow in our prayer life. He prayed that God would relieve the suffering to come, but prayed this only if it would be God's will. He did not wish to be relieved of the suffering if it did not agree with His heavenly Father's will. His disciples were of no comfort to Him during these agonizing hours. They slept through it.

Children rise and sing stanza 2 of "Go to Dark Gethsemane."
Poster 3: Jesus Taken Captive and Tried, is brought forward during the singing of stanza 2.

5. The Old Testament had foretold that Jesus would be betrayed by one of His friends (Psalm 41:9). Judas, that friend, betrayed Jesus for 30 pieces of

silver and turned Him over to the mob waiting to take Him to the high priest for trial.

6. Jesus was tried by the Jewish council, which is called the Sanhedrin. They could not agree on any true accusation so they finally agreed on the false accusation of blasphemy.

7. Christ was arraigned before two courts, the church council and the civil courts of the Romans. The church council had rejected Him as the Messiah and pronounced the verdict, "guilty of death." They were not permitted to execute the death sentence, so Jesus was brought to the Roman civil court.

8. Since Palestine was part of the Roman Empire, a Roman governor was placed over this small country. The Roman governor's name was Pontius Pilate, and he alone had the power to sentence anyone to death. The charges brought against Christ were all false. Pilate admitted that he could not find any fault with Jesus, yet he had Him scourged and finally crucified. Wanting to be held blameless in Jesus' death, he called for water and washed his hands before the mob to show his innocence.

Children rise and sing stanza 3 of "Go to Dark Gethsemane."
Poster 4: Jesus Is Crucified, is brought forward while the children sing stanza 4.

9. Jesus was led to Golgotha to be crucified. He was exhausted and Simon of Cyrene carried his cross. At about 9 a.m. they crucified Him, placing Him in the middle of two notorious criminals. Jesus asked His heavenly Father to forgive those who were executing Him since they didn't realize what they were doing. When Jesus cried out from the cross, "It is finished," hell's gates were closed and heaven's gates were opened for all believing Christians. He died for you and for me.

10. We believe in Christ crucified. With all Christians we confess that through His suffering and death, by crucifixion, He took away all of our sins, thus giving heaven to all who believe in Him as their Savior.

Recessional: "In the Cross of Christ I Glory," TLH, SBH.
Posters remain, and pastor(s), children, and teachers leave the sanctuary.

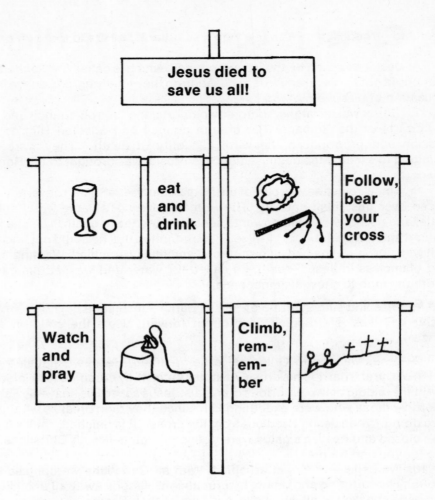

Materials needed

1. sections with captions; background—black, letters—white
2. sections with symbols; background—red, grey, lavender, or magenta, symbols—black
3. ½″ dowels

Note: If children are careful when carrying these posters, construction paper or mat stock paper will work. Poster board is more durable.

6. Christ Is Lord—Praise Him!

Children's Participation

Processional Hymn: "O Savior, Precious Savior," TLH, SBH (congregation). Palm bearers form an arch of palms down the center aisle of the sanctuary. As pastor(s), children, and teachers process into the sanctuary, under the palms, they sing this hymn with the congregation. Five children carry the banners in at the appropriate time and place them at the front of the church.

Banners: Praise Him, Love Him, Thank Him, Crown Him, Serve Him

The Choirs: "Praise Him, Praise Him," *Folk Encounter* (to be sung by the children during the presentation)

"They'll Know We Are Christians by Our Love," *Folk Hymnal for the Now Generation. Folk Encounter*

The Spoken Word: Five banners proclaiming Christ is Lord illustrate the five different crosses as the children explain the meaning of the cross.

1. The most common of all Christian symbols is the cross. The cross reminds us of the suffering and death which our Lord and Savior endured for all people. Various symbols for the cross have been used in church history reminding people of God's greatest Gift. We shall explain five of them and ask that you look at the cross on the banner while it is being explained.

Banner One is brought forward: Christ Is Lord, Praise Him

2. *The Advent Cross* is the cross of the Old Testament, and may be called the prophecy cross. Already in the Garden of Eden, God gave His promise of the Savior. We praise Him for keeping His promise and sending the world a Savior from sin.

3. "I will put enmity between you and the woman, and between your seed and her seed; He shall bruise your head, and you shall bruise His heel" Genesis 3:15.

4. "All you that are righteous, be glad because of what the Lord has done; Praise Him, all you that obey Him" Psalm 33:1.

Children sing "Praise Him," using these words:
Praise Him! Praise Him! All who are God's Children
Christ is Lord, Christ is Lord.
Praise Him! Praise Him! All who are God's children
Christ is Lord, Christ is Lord.

Banner Two is brought forward: Christ Is Lord, Love Him

5. *The Epiphany Cross* is a cross with an orb, which symbolizes how Christ overcame the sin of the world because of His great love for all sinners. We love Him for showing that love for all people.

6. "For God so loved the world that He gave His only Son, that whoever believes in Him should not perish but have eternal life," John 3:16. 1 John 4:19 states: "We love, because He first loved us."

Children sing: Love Him! Love Him! All who are God's children
Christ is Lord, Christ is Lord

Love Him! Love Him! All who are God's children
Christ is Lord, Christ is Lord

Banner Three is brought forward: Christ Is Lord, Thank Him

7. *The Holy Week Cross* is also known as the Passion Cross. The pointed ends on the arms of the cross remind us of Jesus' pain. We thank Him for His suffering and death which He endured for us.

8. "But He was wounded for our transgressions, He was bruised for our iniquities; upon Him was the chastisement that made us whole, and with His stripes we are healed," Isaiah 53:5. "Let us come into His presence with thanksgiving," Psalm 95:2a.

Children sing: Thank Him! Thank Him! All who are God's children
Christ is Lord, Christ is Lord
Thank Him! Thank Him! All who are God's children
Christ is Lord, Christ is Lord

Banner Four is brought forward: Christ Is Lord, Crown Him

9. *The Easter Cross* is the cross of victory over sin and death. Christ is risen and reigns forever in heaven. We crown Him as the victorious King of kings and Lord of lords.

10. "But thanks be to God, who gives us the victory through our Lord Jesus Christ," 1 Corinthians 15:57. Another verse to remember is from Revelation 2:10, which reminds us of our own crown: "Be faithful unto death, and I will give you the crown of life."

Children sing: Crown Him! Crown Him! All who are God's children,
Christ is Lord, Christ is Lord!
Crown Him! Crown Him! All who are God's children
Christ is Lord, Christ is Lord

Banner Five is brought forward: Christ Is Lord, Serve Him

11. The Service Cross is one which can be seen at the front of our church. We at (name of church) receive all the benefits Christ the Lord offers. Therefore we serve Him with a life of service to God and our fellow members of the body of Christ here at (name of church) and elsewhere, in our community, nation, and the world.

12. The following Bible verses remind us of our Christian service: "He did this to prepare all God's people for the work of Christian service, in order to build up the body of Christ" Ephesians 4:12 (TEV). "If one of you wants to be great, he must be the servant of the rest" Mark 10:43. "Help carry one another's burdens, and in this way you will obey the law of Christ" Galatians 6:2. "By love serve one another, Galatians 5:13.

Children sing: Serve Him! Serve Him! All who are God's children
Christ is Lord, Christ is Lord
Serve Him! Serve Him! All who are God's children
Christ is Lord, Christ is Lord

The Silent Prayer: Children encircle the congregation and sing "They'll Know We Are Christians by Our Love."

The Recessional: "Crown Him with Many Crowns," TLH, SBH (congregation). Pastor(s), children, and teachers recess during the hymn. Palm bearers form an arch in the narthex or outside, and people walk out under the palms.

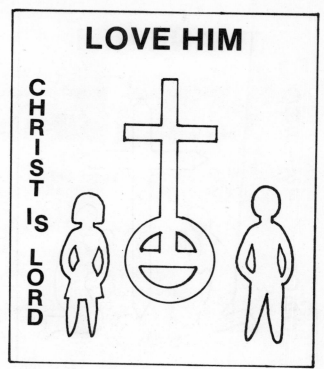

Note: Banner size is determined by church size and display area. Banners can be as small as 24" x 28", or as large as 36" x 48". They could also be used as altar backdrops, or could be made in poster form.

Materials needed

For all banners, black felt for people, black cords and fringes

Praise Him—background, aqua burlap; Christ Is Lord, white felt; Praise Him letters and cross, royal blue felt

Love Him—background, pink or salmon burlap; Christ Is Lord, white felt; Love Him letters and cross and orb, red felt

Thank Him—background, lavender burlap; Christ Is Lord, white letters; Thank Him letters and cross, purple

Crown Him—background, yellow burlap; Christ Is Lord letters and crown, orange felt; Crown Him letters and cross, gold felt

Serve Him—background, light green burlap; Christ Is Lord, white felt; Serve Him letters and cross, bright green or dark green

THANK HIM

CHRIST IS LORD

CROWN HIM

CHRIST IS LORD

SERVE HIM

CHRIST IS LORD

7. Jesus the Promised Messiah and King

Children's Participation

Processional Hymn: "Hosanna, Loud Hosanna," TLH (congregation). Two banner bearers and the pastor(s) lead the procession. The palm bearers hold up palms to form an arch down the center aisle through which the children and teachers then process into the sanctuary.

Banners: Sing Hosanna to Our King
    To Our Redeemer We Give Glory

The Choirs: "Alleluia! Alleluia! Loud Hosannas Now We Raise," *Young Children Sing*

"Riding, Riding," *Sing for Joy* (Two groups sing this song; Group I sings from one side of the church, stanzas 1 and 3; Group II sings sts. 2 and 4 from the other side of the church.)

Note: Another way to do this song is to have the older children sitting in the pews sing sts. 1 and 3. Younger children standing up front can wave the palm branches in rhythm while singing sts. 2 and 4.

The Spoken Word: Children read the Gospel lesson in words taken from the Egermeier Bible Story Book.

1. A time of great excitement was on. People were flocking out of the city gate and hurrying along the road that led down the valley and up the slope of Mount Olivet, just outside of Jerusalem. They were rushing out to meet Jesus, of whom they had heard such great things.

2. Many of these people were strangers in Jerusalem. They had come to attend the feast of the Passover, and they had heard about the wonderful miracles Jesus performed. . . . Many of the people took branches of palm trees with which to wave a welcome when they should meet Him.

3. On the morning of that same day Jesus had sent two of His disciples to a village near Bethany to loose a colt which they should find tied. He had told them to bring this colt to Him, and if the owners should question why they untied the colt they should answer, "The Lord has need of this colt today." The disciples had gone and found the colt tied by the roadside, and they had told the owners the message which Jesus sent. And the owners let them take the colt and bring it to Jesus.

4. Then the disciples had spread their garments on the colt's back and had set Jesus on it, while others threw their jackets along the road for Jesus to ride over. And as the crowd from Jerusalem came near to the Mount of Olives, the company which followed from Bethany began to shout, "Blessed is the King who is coming in the name of the Lord! Peace in heaven and glory in the highest!"

5. The people who came out of Jerusalem met Jesus and His disciples on the slope of the Mount of Olives. They heard those who followed Jesus shout praises to Him, and they too waved their palms and rejoiced, saying, "Hosanna, Blessed is the King of Israel who comes in the name of the Lord!"

Some threw their palms in the road for Him to ride over, and all along the highway they stood, rejoicing greatly and praising God.

6. In the crowd were some Pharisees who had not come to rejoice but to find fault. When they heard the people shouting they came to Jesus and said, "Master, cause these to cease shouting." But Jesus answered, "If these should be still the stones by the roadside would immediately cry out." Jesus knew the time had come when the prophecy of Zechariah should be fulfilled, for Zechariah had said concerning this very time: "Rejoice greatly, O daughter of Zion; shout O daughter of Jerusalem; behold your King comes to you; He is just and having salvation; lowly and riding upon a colt."

7. So the crowd passed on through the gate into the city, and Jesus rode up Mount Moriah, where the temple stood. And as He went, the people before and behind cried out aloud, "Hosanna to the Son of David." And the people in the city were stirred with the excitement. They came hurrying into the streets to ask, "What is the meaning of all this? Who is this King you are bringing? And the multitude answered, "This is Jesus, the Prophet from Nazareth, of Galilee."

8. Then Jesus entered the temple and looked about upon the things there. Everyone was eager to see Jesus. The blind and the lame came to Him in the temple, and He healed them there.

9. And little children came singing, "Hosanna to the Son of David!" No doubt they had heard the glad songs of the grown people who had come with Jesus from the Mount of Olives, and they, too, wished to praise this great man, who took little ones in His arms and blessed them.

10. The chief priests and scribes in the temple saw Jesus heal the blind and the lame, and they heard the children sing His praises. They were angered by these things, for they saw that every day the multitudes were becoming more excited about this Jesus.

11. They came to Jesus and asked, "Do you hear what these children are saying?" And Jesus replied, "Yes, I hear them. Have you never read these words in the Scriptures, 'Out of the mouths of little children Thou hast perfected praise'?"

The Recessional: "Ride On, Ride On, in Majesty," TLH, SBH. Palm bearers form an arch of palms in the narthex so all go out under the palms. Pastor(s), children, and teachers recess while the congregation sings this hymn.

Materials needed

Sing Hosanna to Our King
1. lavender felt—background
2. purple felt—cross, sing, to, our
3. yellow-orange or yellow felt—crown, hosanna, King
4. fringe and cord—yellow-orange or yellow

To Our Redeemer We Give Glory
1. lavender felt—background
2. purple felt—cross, to, our, we, give
3. yellow-orange or yellow felt—star of David, Redeemer, glory
4. fringe and cord—yellow-orange or yellow

8. Jesus Lives and We Shall Too

Children's Participation

Processional Hymn: "I Know that My Redeemer Lives," TLH, SBH (congregation). Pastor(s), children, and teachers enter the sanctuary.

The Choirs: "Jesus Christ Is Risen Today," *Young Children Sing* (younger children)

"Come, All People, Raise Your Voices," *Children Sing*, Book 3 (older children)

The Spoken Word: An acrostic, "Easter, Jesus Lives," will be told by young children. Each child places his letter card on the display board, completing the design. If you do not wish to use a display board, make larger letter cards. Have the children line up in front of the church and hold up their letter card as they speak.

1. *E* is for early. The Bible tells us that it was very early on Sunday morning when the Marys and Salome went to the grave of Jesus.
2. *A* is for angel. They wondered who would roll away the large stone from the grave. When they arrived it was rolled away and an angel was standing by the grave.
3. *S* is for spices. The women had come with spices to anoint the body of Jesus. They didn't need the spices, because Jesus was alive.
4. *T* is for tell. The angel told the ladies that Jesus was alive. They were to tell His disciples that Jesus had risen.
5. *E* is for Easter. Today we celebrate Easter because Jesus is our everliving Lord and King.
6. *R* is for risen. Jesus is risen from the dead. He lives. We greet each other on Easter by saying, "He is risen."

7. *J* is for John. As soon as John and Peter heard the news from Mary Magdalene, they ran to the tomb. The Bible says that John ran faster than Peter and reached the grave before Peter.
8. *E* is for exalted. Jesus is our exalted Savior. He showed that He is the exalted Lord by conquering death for us.
9. *S* is for see. The angel told the women at the grave, "He is not here; for He has risen, as He said. Come, *see* the place where He lay."
10. *U* is for us. Easter is good news for all of us. Jesus said, "Because I live, you shall live also."
11. *S* is for Scripture. The Scriptures tell us that Jesus rose on Easter morning. We believe it because the Scriptures are God speaking to us.

12. *L* is for life. God gave each of us life. Because of sin in the world life is taken away through death. But Jesus tells us in the Bible that there really is life after death. That life will be in heaven with Him.
13. *I* is for I believe. Each one of us must believe the Easter message for himself. I believe it, do you?
14. *V* is for victory. Jesus won the victory over sin, death, and the devil. He told us that we, too, are the winners or victors over these.
15. *E* is for eternal life. We should all be happy Christians because Easter means that all of us who believe in Jesus as our Savior have eternal life.
16. *S* is for Sunday. Jesus rose from the dead on the first day of the week.

That's why the early Christians chose Sunday to have their church service. Each Sunday should be a reminder to us of what happened on that first Easter. Let's all worship our risen Lord every Sunday.

Recessional: "Jesus Lives! The Victory's Won," TLH. The pastor(s), children, and teachers leave the sanctuary during the joyful singing of this hymn.

Materials needed

1. one display board about 3'x4', black burlap is beautiful for this
2. construction paper the color of the display board for the letter cards
3. 3" or 4" letter patterns and construction paper
4. orange fadeless art paper or construction paper for the Easter cross
5. yellow sunbeams
6. yellow-green for the branches

9. Appearances of the Risen Savior

Children's Participation

Processional Hymn: "Jesus Christ Is Risen Today, Alleluia," TLH, SBH (congregation). The pastor(s) will lead the children and teachers into the sanctuary singing this hymn with the congregation.

The Choirs: "Christ the Lord Is Risen Today," TCH, *Joyful Sounds* (older children)
"He Is Lord," *Sing to the Lord, Folk Encounter* (younger children)

The Spoken Word: The children will have prepared write-on slides of illustrations of each account; these will be projected while selected children read the numbered selections from the Bible.

APPEARANCE TO MARY MAGDALENE

Slide 1 is projected

1. The Bible tells us that Jesus first appeared to Mary Magdalene. This account is recorded in John 20:11-18. We read it here from the *Good News Bible, The Bible in Today's English Version.* (11) Mary stood crying outside the tomb. While she was still crying, she bent over and looked in the tomb (12) and saw two angels there dressed in white, sitting where the body of Jesus had been, one at the head and the other at the feet.

2. (13) "Woman, why are you crying?" they asked her. She answered, "They have taken my Lord away, and I do not know where they have put Him!"

Slide 2 is projected

3. (14) Then she turned around and saw Jesus standing there; but she did not know that it was Jesus. (15) "Woman, why are you crying?" Jesus asked her. "Who is it that you are looking for?" She thought He was the gardener, so she said to Him, "If you took Him away, sir, tell me where you have put Him, and I will go and get Him." (16) Jesus said to her, "Mary!"

4. She turned toward Him and said in Hebrew, "Rabboni!" (This means "Teacher"). (17) "Do not hold on to Me," Jesus told her, "because I have not yet gone back up to the Father. But go to My brothers and tell them that I am returning to Him who is My Father, and their Father, my God and their God." (18) So Mary Magdalene went and told the disciples that she had seen the Lord and related to them what He had told her.

APPEARANCE TO THE OTHER WOMEN

Slide 3 is projected

5. This account is recorded in Matthew 28:5-10. (5) The angel spoke to the women. "You must not be afraid," he said, "I know you are looking for Jesus, who was crucified. (6) He is not here; He has been raised, just as He said. Come here and see the place where He was lying. (7) Go quickly now, and tell His disciples, 'He has been raised from death, and now He is going to

Galilee ahead of you; there you will see Him!' Remember what I have told you."

Slide 4 is projected

6. (8) So they left the tomb in a hurry, afraid and yet filled with joy, and ran to tell His disciples. (9) Suddenly Jesus met them and said, "Peace be with you." They came up to Him, took hold of His feet, and worshiped Him. (10) "Do not be afraid," Jesus said to them. "Go and tell My brothers to go to Galilee, and there they will see Me."

APPEARANCE TO TWO DISCIPLES ON THE WAY TO EMMAUS

Slide 5 is projected

7. We find the account of the walk to Emmaus written in Luke 24:13-32. (13) On that same day two of Jesus' followers were going to a village named Emmaus, about seven miles from Jerusalem, (14) and they were talking to each other about all the things that had happened.

Slide 6 is projected

8. (15) As they talked and discussed, Jesus himself drew near and walked along with them; (16) they saw Him, but somehow did not recognize Him. (17) Jesus said to them, "What are you talking about to each other, as you walk along?"

9. They stood still with sad faces. (18) One of them, named Cleopas, asked Him, "Are You the only visitor in Jerusalem who doesn't know the things that have been happening there these last few days?" (19) "What things?" He asked.

10. "The things that happened to Jesus of Nazareth," they answered. "This Man was a prophet and was considered by God and by all the people to be powerful in everything He said and did.

11. (20) Our chief priests and rulers handed Him over to be sentenced to death, and He was crucified. (21) And we had hoped that He would be the one who was going to set Israel free! Besides all that, this is now the third day since it happened.

12. (22) Some of the women of our group surprised us; they went at dawn to the tomb, (23) but could not find His body. They came back saying they had seen a vision of angels who told them that He is alive. (24) Some of our group went to the tomb and found it exactly as the women had said, but they did not see Him."

13. (25) Then Jesus said to them, "How foolish you are, how slow you are to believe everything the prophets said! (26) Was it not necessary for the Messiah to suffer these things and then to enter His glory?" (27) And Jesus explained to them what was said about Himself in all the Scriptures, beginning with the books of Moses and the writings of all the prophets.

Slide 7 is projected

14. (28) As they came near the village to which they were going, Jesus acted as if He were going farther; (29) but they held Him back saying, "Stay with us; the day is almost over and it is getting dark." So He went in to stay with them.

Slide 8 is projected

15. (30) He sat down to eat with them, took the bread, and said the blessing;

then He broke the bread and gave it to them. (31) Then their eyes were opened and they recognized Him, but He disappeared from their sight. (32) They said to each other, "Wasn't it like a fire burning in us when He talked to us on the road and explained the Scriptures to us?"

APPEARANCE TO HIS DISCIPLES (the eleven)

Slide 9 is projected

16. We read about this appearance in John 20:19-23. (19) It was late that Sunday evening, and the disciples were gathered together behind locked doors, because they were afraid of the Jewish authorities. Then Jesus came and stood among them. "Peace be with you," He said. (20) After saying this, He showed them His hands and His side. The disciples were filled with joy at seeing the Lord.

17. (21) Jesus said to them again, "Peace be with you. As the Father sent Me, so I send you." (22) Then He breathed on them and said, "Receive the Holy Spirit. (23) If you forgive people's sins, they are forgiven; if you do not forgive them, they are not forgiven."

18. The glorious Easter message, "Christ is risen indeed!" is as true as it is true that God made heaven and earth, and lets the sun rise every morning. These appearances of Jesus certainly will strengthen our faith; we know that many truthful witnesses saw our risen Lord. He is risen!

The Recessional: "I Know that My Redeemer Lives," TLH, SBH. The pastor(s), children, and teachers leave the sanctuary joyfully singing this hymn with the congregation.

Note: Make one or two slides to test for distance, size, and intensity before asking the children to make the slides. You may want to have art students serve on a committee to make the slides.

Materials needed

1. Kodak Ektagraphic Write-On Slides (12-18)
2. colored art pencils
3. scrap paper for children to use to practice

10. The Great Commission and the Ascension of Jesus

Children's Participation

The Processional Hymn: "Spread, Oh, Spread, Thou Mighty Word," TLH, SBH (congregation). One poster bearer, and six flag bearers will lead pastor(s), children, and teachers into the sanctuary. If you wish you may add other poles of flags to put in the sanctuary. Add the names of the countries.

Poster: King of Kings

The Choirs: "Oh, He's King of Kings," *Joyful Sounds* (younger children)
"Draw Us to Thee," *Joyful Sounds* (older children)

The Spoken Word: The Gospel lesson will be told by the children in words taken from *Concordia Bible Story Book:* the Great Commission and the account of Jesus' return to His home in heaven.

1. Shortly before Jesus ascended into heaven, He met with His disciples on a mountain in Galilee. He said to them, "All power in heaven and on earth has been given to Me. Go therefore and make disciples of all nations, baptizing them in the name of the Father and of the Son and of the Holy Spirit, teaching them to do everything I have commanded you. And remember, I am with you always, even to the end of the world."

2. On the last of the 40 days Jesus appeared once more to His disciples, this time in Jerusalem. He told them to stay in Jerusalem until the Holy Spirit had come and given them the power they would need to do their preaching. He said, "John baptized with water, but in a few days you will be baptized with the Holy Spirit."

3. Then Jesus led His disciples out of Jerusalem and along a road that went toward Bethany and the mount of Olives. On the mount Jesus stopped. Here the disciples asked Jesus whether He was going to drive out the Romans, who were ruling over the land, and set up the kingdom of Israel once more.

4. Jesus did not answer this question. He simple told His disciples that it was not their business to know what the heavenly Father was going to do on earth at any time. Jesus wanted the thoughts of the disciples to be on their work.

5. He continued His instruction by saying, "You shall receive power when the Holy Spirit has come upon you. And you shall tell the truth about Me to all people—in Jerusalem, in Judea, in Samaria, and to the ends of the earth."

6. When Jesus had said this, He lifted up His hands and blessed the disciples. While He was blessing them, He began to rise from the ground. The disciples watched Him rise and worshiped Him.

7. Soon a bright cloud hid Him from their sight. Jesus had returned to heaven. But the disciples kept looking up to the place where they had last seen Him.

8. Suddenly two angels dressed in white stood beside them. The angels said, "Men of Galilee, why do you stand there looking up to heaven? This Jesus, who was taken from you into heaven, will come again in the same way as you saw Him go to heaven."

9. The disciples were glad when they heard this. They worshiped God and went back to Jerusalem with great joy.

The Recessional Hymn: "Hark! the Voice of Jesus Crying," TLH, SBH. Pastor(s), children, and teachers recess from the sanctuary.

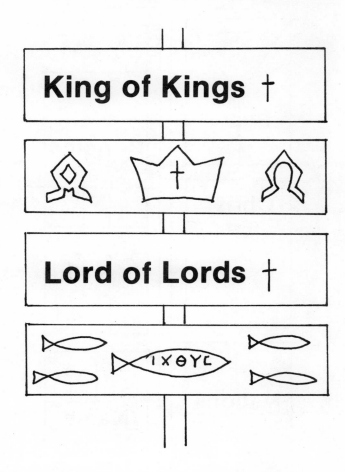

Materials needed

1. Four bright colors of poster board, each 28"x11"
2. black construction paper for letters
3. white construction paper for cutouts

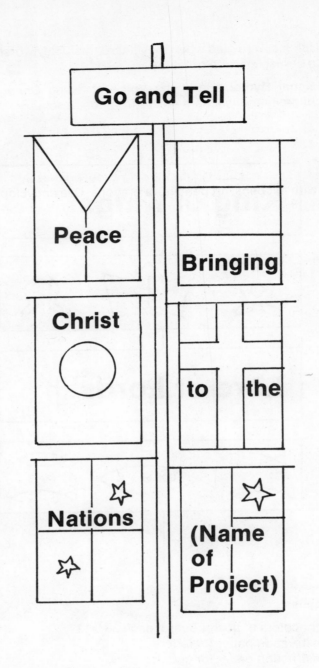

Go and Tell

Peace

Christ

Nations

Bringing

to the

(Name of Project)

How to Use the Flags

The insignias and symbols of the flags in this book are scaled for two sizes. The small designs are for 7"x11" and fit on a ditto. They are good on posters and banners and can be used with any mission service. They can also be used with mission fairs, as well as in classrooms, or Sunday school departments. Children can make booklets when studying about our mission fields. They can be colored with felt pens, art pencils, or crayons. Use encyclopedias for color guides. When transparencies are made of this size, you can make posters 22"x28", and some even larger.

The larger patterns are scaled for posters, 14"x22", or one-half a regular-size poster board. They can also be used on 12"x18" construction paper with some adjustments. Banners, which can be carried as real flags, can also be made. With the help of transparencies, theater-sized posters of any of these countries can be made if you wish to feature a special country as the 'Hearts for Jesus' projects often do. Construction paper or fadeless art paper works best on the posters. Make the patterns for the flags and let the children make the posters, under your supervision. Children should be reminded to treat flags with respect, even when they are posters. The large poster flags can serve as background for titles of mission projects.

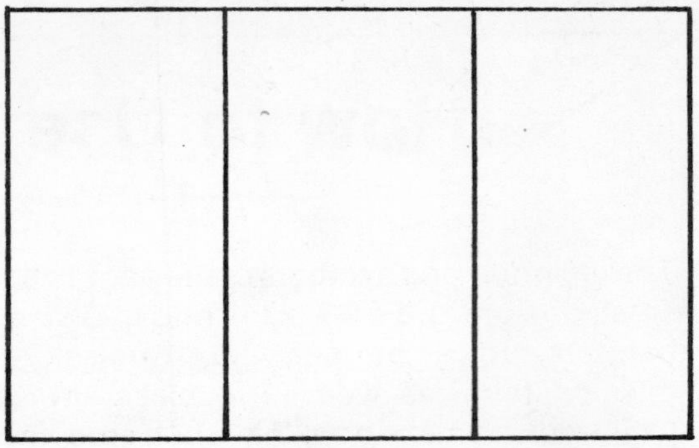

Argentina, Honduras, Venezuela
W. Germany, Ghana, Paraguay
El Salvador, India

Mexico, Guatemala, Nigeria
France, Belgium

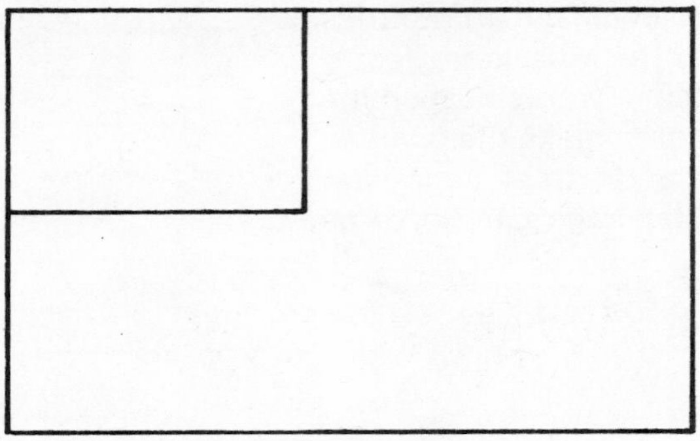

Nationalist China

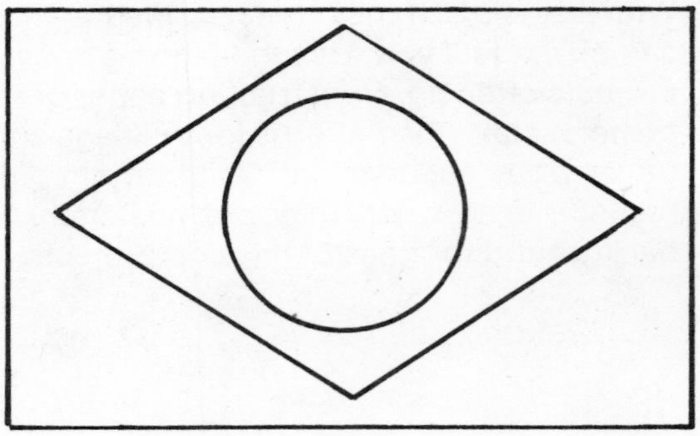

Brazil

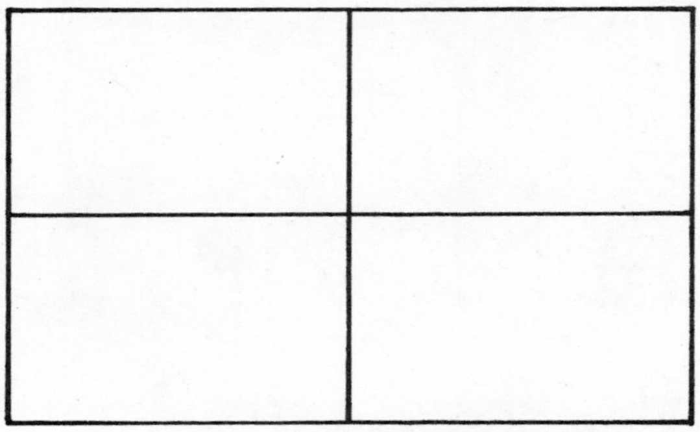

Panama

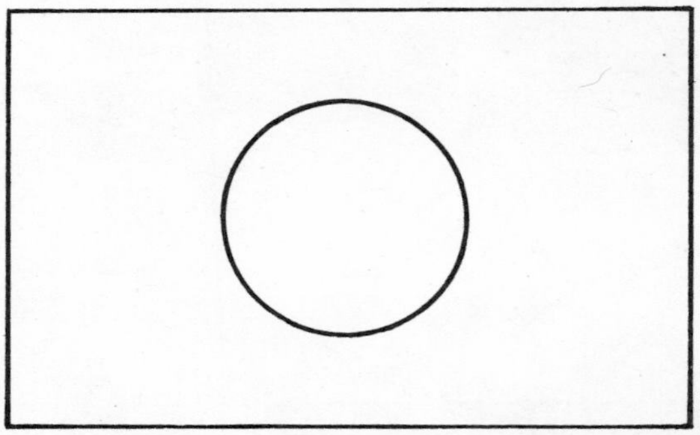

Japan

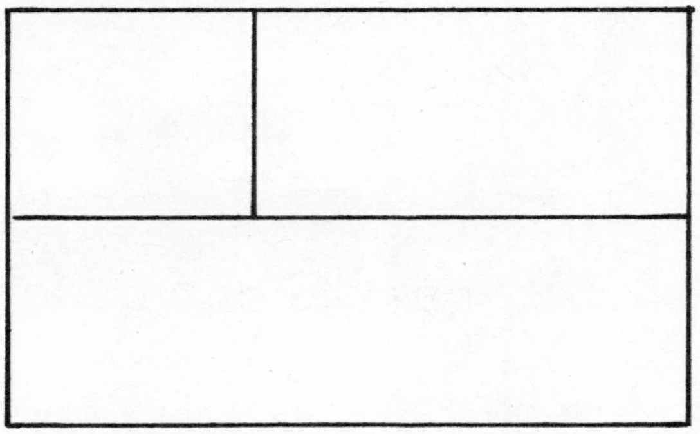

Chile

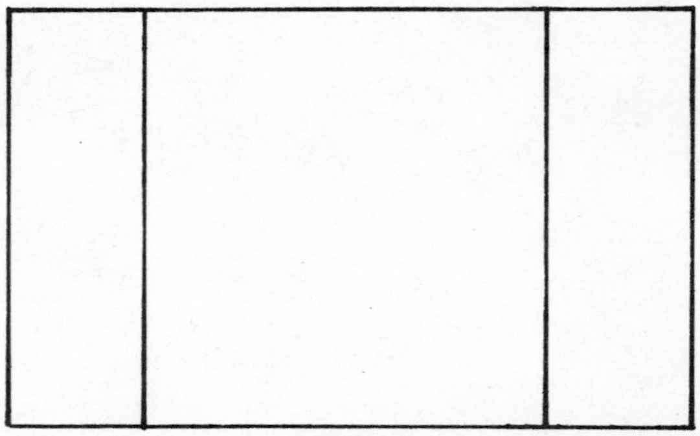

Canada

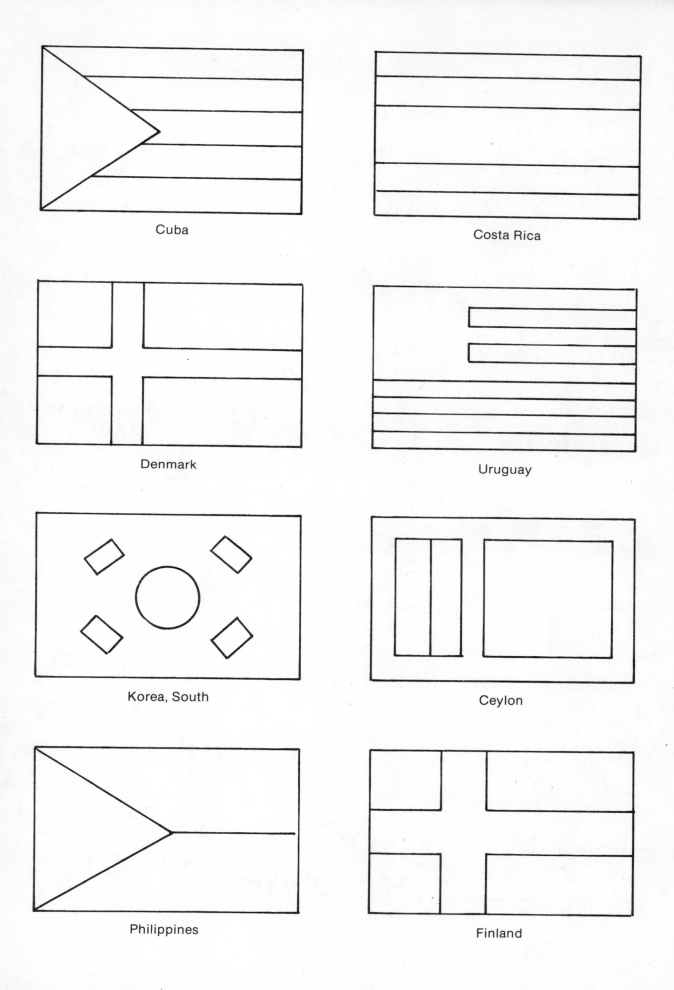

Cuba

Costa Rica

Denmark

Uruguay

Korea, South

Ceylon

Philippines

Finland

Guatemala

Mexico

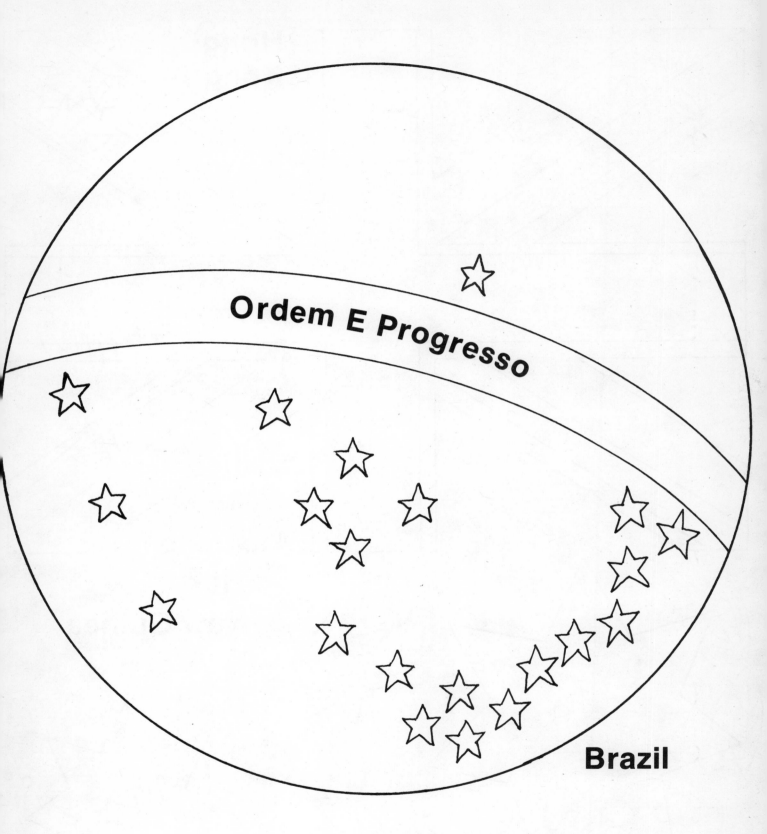

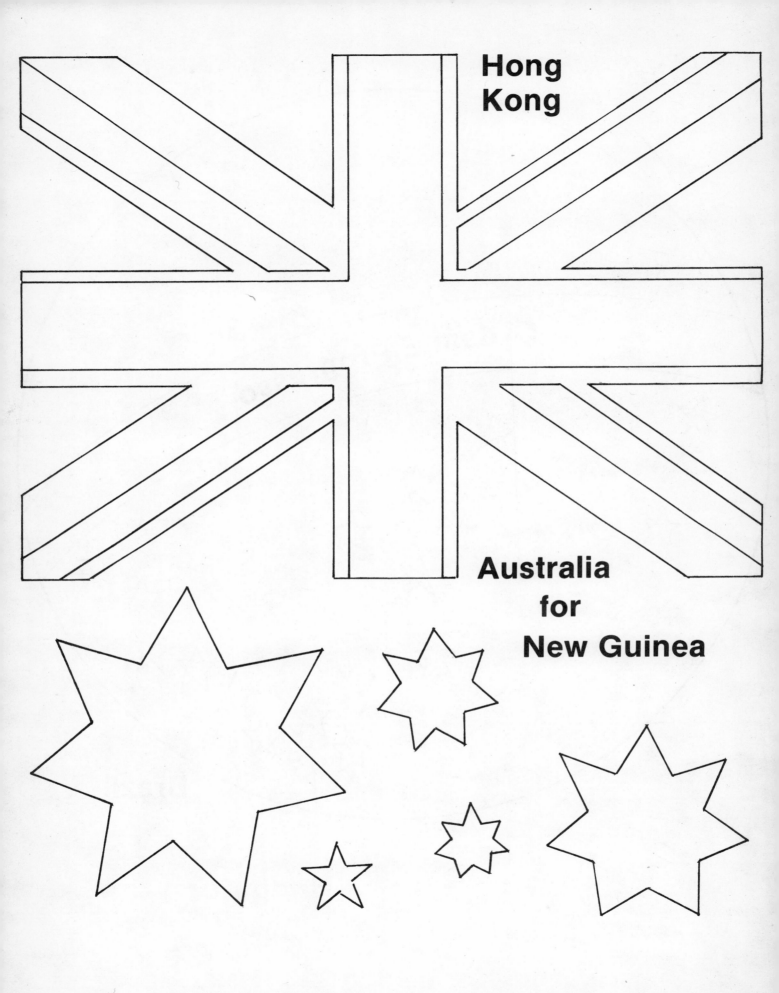

Hong
Kong

Australia
for
New Guinea

Brazil

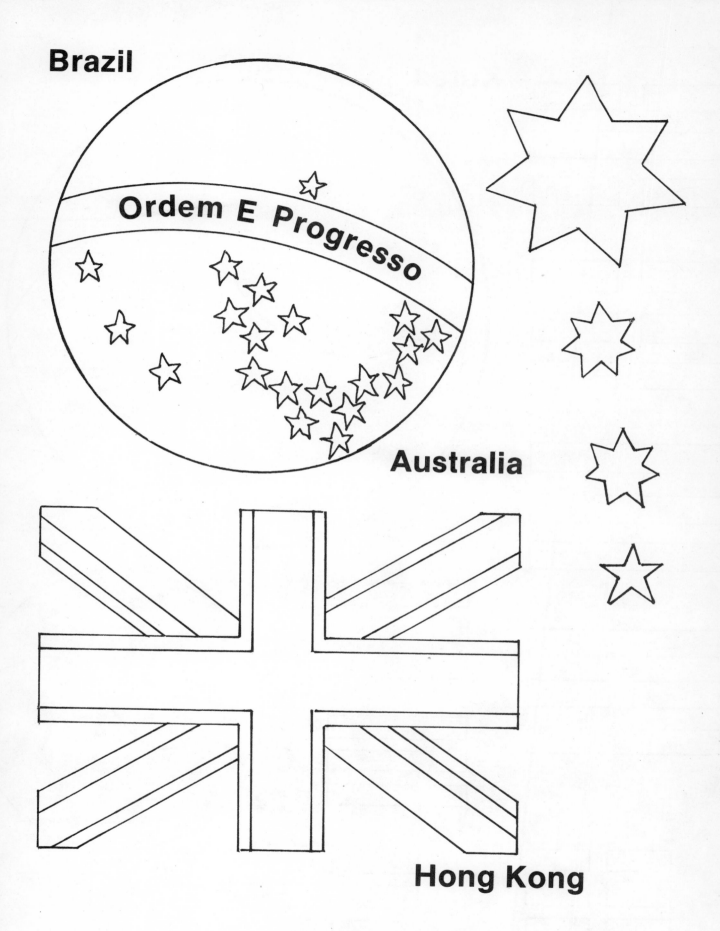

Ordem E Progresso

Australia

Hong Kong

Korea

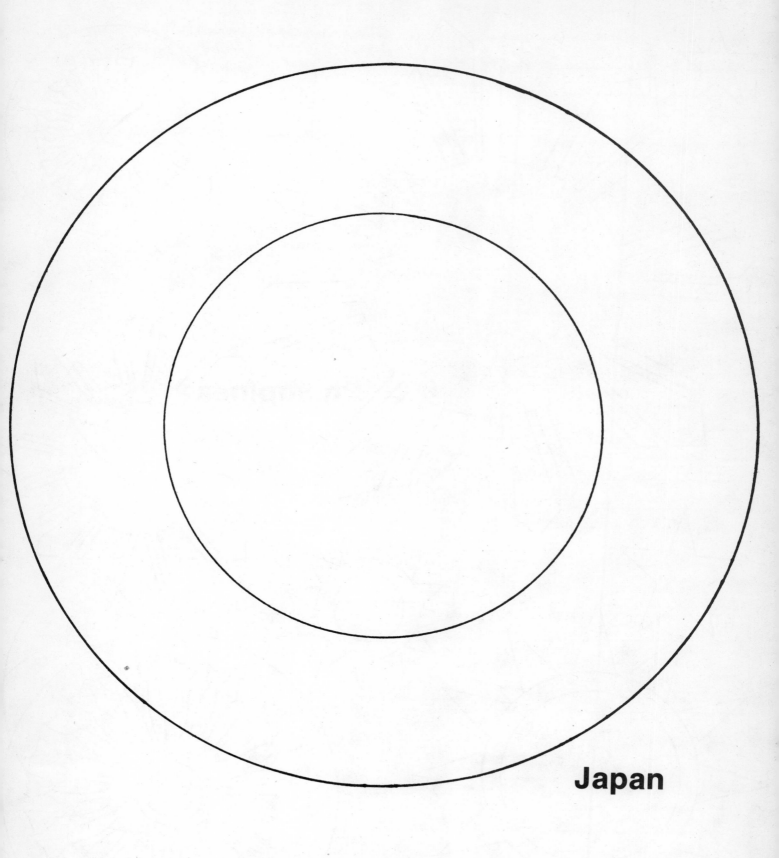

Japan

Philippines

Nationalist China

India

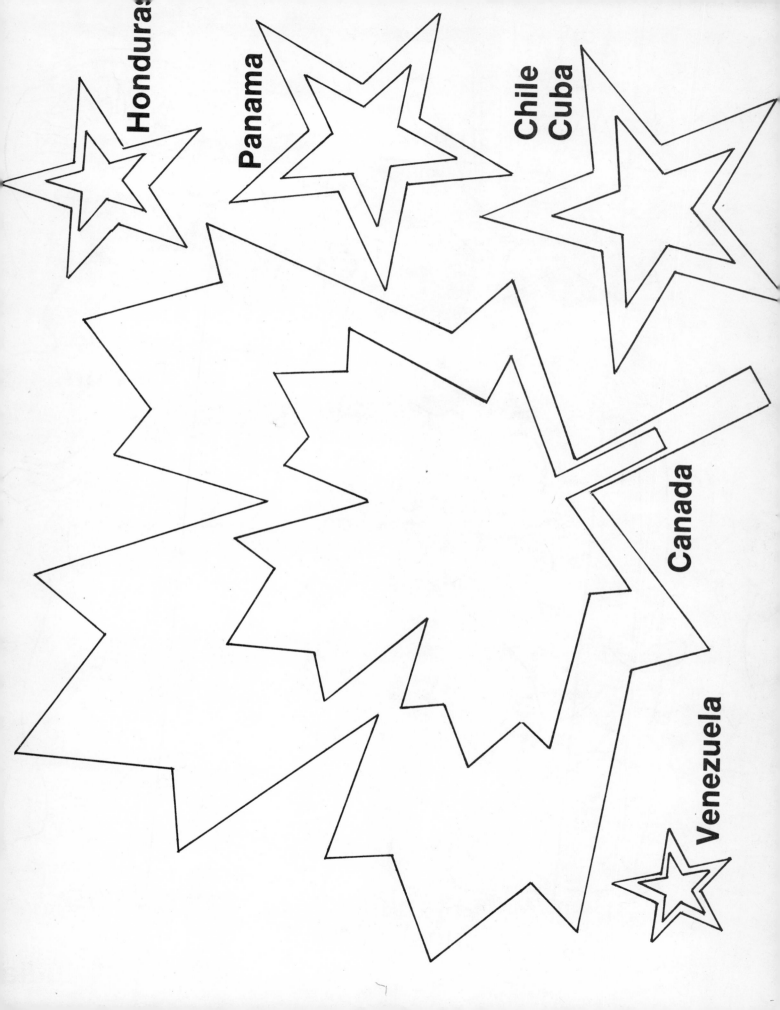

Honduras

Panama

Chile
Cuba

Canada

Venezuela

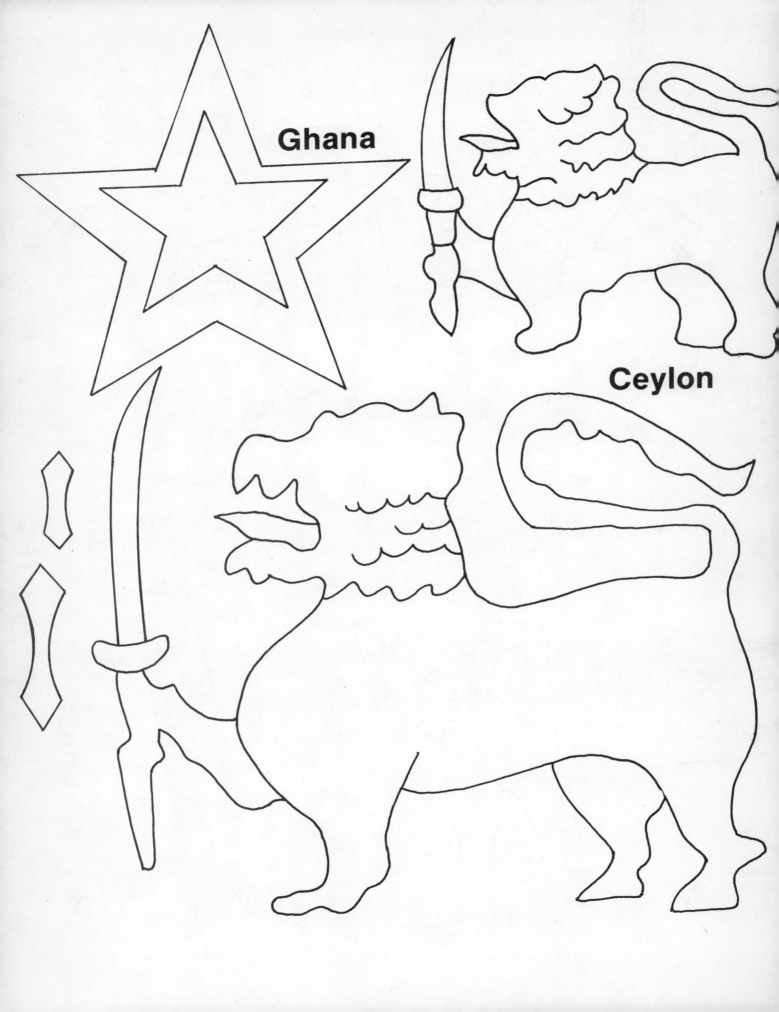

Ghana

Ceylon

Uruguay

Argentina

11. Heaven Is Our Wonderful Home

Children's Participation

Processional: "Jerusalem the Golden," TLH, SBH. Banner bearers, pastor(s), children, and teachers process into the sanctuary singing this beautiful hymn with the congregation.

Banner: Come Lord Jesus

The Choirs: "Children of the Heavenly Father," *Joyful Sounds* (older children)
"Swing Low, Sweet Chariot," *Joyful Sounds* (all children)
"Jesus, Lead Thou On," *Joyful Sounds* (older children encircle the older congregation and sing stanzas 1 and 4)

The Spoken Word: The children read their speaking parts, describing the visions the apostle John saw, recorded in the Book of Revelation. The children's parts are taken from the *Concordia Bible Story Book.*

Introduction: After the ascension of Jesus the apostles spread the Good News in countries of Asia Minor and southern Europe. God blessed their work and several congregations were formed. John lived longer than the other apostles, and under the rule of the Romans was exiled to the island of Patmos. He was not alone because God was with him. Here John was permitted to see visions of what would happen to the followers of Jesus, and also glimpses of heaven. We want to tell you about some of the visions of heaven which John saw, which are recorded in the Book of Revelation.

1. On a Sunday, while sitting on a high rock overlooking the sea, John heard a loud voice behind him. When he turned to see who was speaking, he saw seven golden lampstands and Jesus in the midst of them. Jesus wore a long robe with a band of gold around His chest.

2. In His right hand He held seven stars. His head and hair were as white as snow, and His eyes like flames of fire. His face was as bright as the brightest sunshine, and His voice sounded like the rushing of many waters.

3. John fell down as if dead, for he was overcome with fear. But Jesus touched him and said, "Have no fear. I am the One who died, and now I am alive forevermore." . . .

4. Next John saw an open door through which he could look into heaven. What a wonderful sight! God was seated on a great throne. Around the throne was a rainbow of one color, bright green. In front of it was what looked like a sea of clear glass.

5. Out of the throne came flashes of lightning, the sound of voices, and peals of thunder. Round about it were smaller thrones. On them sat 24 elders. They were dressed in white and wore crowns of gold on their heads. On each side of the throne stood four living creatures, each having six wings. Day and night, without ever resting, they praised God, saying, "Holy, holy, holy is the Lord God Almighty, who was and is and is to come." . . .

6. Then all the creatures of the earth and the vast chorus of holy angels joined the elders and all the believers who had died and gone to heaven in a tremendous hymn of praise that would continue into all eternity. They sang,

"Worthy is the lamb who was slain to receive power and riches, wisdom and might, honor and glory and blessing!" . . .

7. Last of all John saw himself as being carried away by an angel to a high mountain. There the angel showed him the city of God, or New Jerusalem, coming down out of heaven. A high wall surrounded the city of God. The wall had 12 foundations, and on them were the names of the twelve apostles.

8. Each of the 12 gates in the wall was a single pearl. The city itself was made of pure gold, and the glory of God filled it with a wonderful light. People of every nation lived in this city. God lived with them, and they were His people. There were no tears in their eyes, for in the city of God pain, sorrow, and unhappiness, even death, would forever be gone.

9. This was a vision of heaven. After John had seen all of the visions, he fell down on his knees to worship the angel through whom God had brought them to him. But the angel said, "Do not worship me, for I am only a servant. Worship God instead."

10. Then Jesus spoke. He said, "Let all who desire to live in the heavenly home and enjoy its blessings say, 'Come.'" John wanted very much to have the blessings of heaven, and he longed for the day when Jesus would return and take him there. So when Jesus said to him, "Surely I am coming soon," John prayed, "Come, Lord Jesus."

Recessional: "For All the Saints," TLH, SBH. Banner bearer, pastor(s), children, and teachers leave the sanctuary singing this hymn with the congregation.

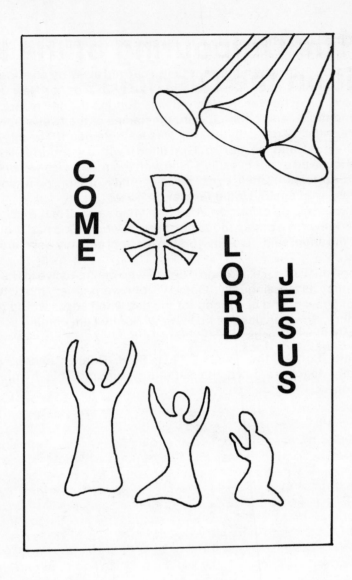

Materials needed

1. light blue felt or burlap for background
2. gold trumpets
3. navy blue or avocado green people
4. maroon, wine, or dark red for the ChiRho
5. bright blue or royal blue letters
6. gold glitter if you like

Note: You may want to use more yellow, yellow-orange, light gold, light blue, and avocado green background. Many color combinations will make a beautiful banner.

12. The Outpouring of the Holy Spirit on the Disciples

Children's Participation

Processional: "Holy Ghost, with Light Divine," TLH ("Holy Spirit, Truth Divine"), SBH (congregtion). One banner bearer will lead the pastor(s), children, and teachers into the house of worship.

Banner: Pour Out Your Spirit

The Choirs: "Spirit Divine, Attend Our Prayers," *Joyful Sounds* (older children)
"I Believe in God Above," *Sing to the Lord* (younger children)
"Pentecost Prayer," *Children Sing,* Book 2 (all children)

The Spoken Word: In place of the Epistle lesson for Pentecost, the children may read the account of "The Coming of the Holy Spirit," as found in the *Concordia Bible Story Book.*

1. Ten days after Jesus returned to heaven the Israelites celebrated one of their important church festivals. It was called Pentecost, or feast of the Harvest. The purpose of the feast was to thank and praise God for all the good things that grew in the fields, which had been gathered and stored away.

2. A large number of people came to Jerusalem for the feast. Many of them were from foreign lands, and they spoke a variety of dialects and languages. Some were from the neighborhood of Persia, others from Egypt, still others from Arabia, from faraway Rome, and from other places. The streets of Jerusalem were crowded with them as they made their way to the temple to bring a thank offering and praise the Lord for His goodness.

3. Early in the morning on the day of Pentecost 120 followers of Jesus, including the apostles and Mary, the mother of Jesus, were together in one place. They were waiting for the Holy Spirit to come, whom Jesus had promised to send.

4. About nine o'clock, while the disciples were praying, there was a strange noise. It sounded like a mighty blast of wind. It came down from heaven and went to the room in which the disciples were gathered, filling it completely.

5. The people in Jerusalem heard the noise. Greatly excited, they came running, wondering what had happened. When they arrived at the place where the disciples were staying, they saw something that looked like a little flame of fire, shaped like a tongue, on the head of each one of them. The little flames were the sign that the Holy Spirit had come to live in their hearts and give them power to do the work that God wanted them to do.

6. The Holy Spirit made the disciples brave and eager to go out and tell people about Jesus the Savior. He also made them able to speak languages they could not speak before. Now they could tell the people of various nations about Jesus the Savior, using their own language.

7. The disciples lost no time in making use of the power they had just received. They stepped before the crowd around them and began speaking about the mighty deeds of God.

8. The Jews from other lands were amazed when they heard the disciples speaking their languages. They said to one another, "Are not these men from Galilee? How is it that we hear them telling about the wonderful works of God in our languages?" Puzzled and confused, they asked, "What does this mean?"

9. Those who said these things were God-fearing people. But there also were some scoffers in the crowd. They mocked the disciples, saying, "These men have drunk too much new wine."

10. When Peter heard this mocking, he boldly stepped before the crowd to preach a sermon. Speaking loudly so that all might hear, Peter said, "Men of Judea and all who live in Jerusalem, listen to me. These men are not drunk, as you suppose. What has happened here today was foretold by the prophet Joel, who said, 'God promises that He will pour out His Spirit upon people in every land.'"

11. "Now," Peter continued, "that prophecy has been fulfilled. The Holy Spirit has come to us today." Then Peter told about Christ's death and resurrection. "Jesus indeed was to die according to God's plan and fore-knowledge," Peter said, "but it was you who took Jesus, the Son of God, and by the hands of lawless men put Him to death. But God has raised Him from the dead . . . ."

12. When the people heard this, their consciences troubled them. Realizing that Jesus, whom they had crucified, was their Lord and Savior, they said to Peter and the other disciples, "Brothers, what shall we do?"

13. Peter answered, "Repent of your sins and be baptized, every one of you, in the name of Jesus Christ for the forgiveness of your sins. Then the Holy Spirit will be given to you."

14. The people who believed the Word of God which Peter spoke were baptized. There were about 3,000 of them. These 3,000 formed the first Christian congregation.

15. In the days that followed, the disciples kept on preaching about Jesus, and every day the Holy Spirit led more people to faith in Him, thus adding to the number of believers.

Recessional: "Come, Holy Ghost, Creator Blest," TLH. "Come, Gracious Spirit, Heavenly Dove," SBH. Banner bearer, pastor(s), children, and teachers leave the sanctuary during the singing of this hymn.

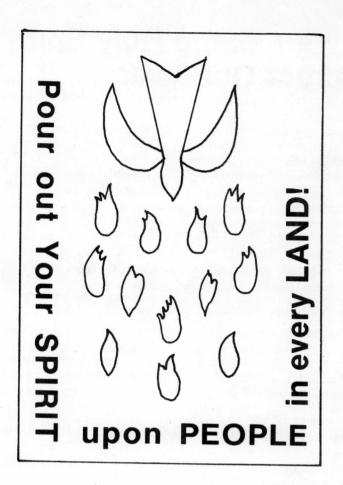

Materials needed

1. background—black burlap or felt
2. twelve flames for the apostles—red and red-orange felt
3. dove—white felt
4. letters—yellow felt
5. fringe—white
6. cord—black or white

13. We Ask the Holy Spirit to Direct Our Lives

Children's Participation

Processional: "Come, Holy Ghost, in Love," TLH, SBH (congregation). A banner bearer leads the procession, with the pastor(s), children, and teachers following.

Banner: Let the Spirit Direct Your Lives

The Choirs: "Spirit of God in the Clear Running Water," *Folk Hymnal for the Now Generation* (all children)

"They'll Know We Are Christians by Our Love," *Folk Hymnal for the Now Generation* (all children)

One of the selections may be sung during the offering.

The Spoken Word: Six children of Group I and nine children in Group II approach the front and form semicircles and present the following recitations.

GROUP I

1. On Pentecost we remember how the disciples received the Holy Spirit in a special way. This gift from God equipped them for the great work they were to do as His witnesses.

2. The Holy Spirit is the third Person of the Holy Trinity. He is God. Other names the Bible gives to the Holy Spirit are: Counselor, Comforter, Paraclete, Advocate, and Holy Ghost.

3. Jesus had told His disciples He would send the Comforter. The original meaning of Comforter was "one who makes strong." He certainly made the disciples strong in their faith and zeal to do the Lord's work.

4. The Holy Spirit came to us through Holy Baptism. He brought us to faith in Jesus and keeps us in faith. The Holy Spirit leads us to do God's will and live God's way. He makes us strong in faith.

5. In Galatians 5:22-23 we read about the fruits which the Holy Spirit leads His people to produce, "But the fruit of the Spirit is love, joy, peace, patience, kindness, goodness, faithfulness, gentleness, and self-control."

6. If we ask God for His Spirit, He will give each of us His Spirit so we can produce such fruit in our lives. We now ask you to pray with us as the children in Group II lead us.

GROUP II

1. Holy Spirit, give us love, love for You and our neighbor.
2. Comforter, bring peace to our homes, church and nation.
3. Paraclete of God, let our joy know no end.
4. Counselor of God, teach us patience in all that we do.
5. God the Holy Ghost, help us to experience kindness in our dealings with people.
6. God the Holy Spirit, allow goodness to be seen in our relations with others.

7. God the Comforter, make us strong so that faithfulness may be one of our traits.

8. God the Counselor, lead us to be gentle to one another.

9. God the Holy Spirit, teach us self-control. We ask that You control our thoughts, words, and deeds. Hear our prayer for Jesus' sake. Amen

The Recessional: "Creator Spirit, by Whose Aid," TLH, SBH. The banner bearer, pastor(s), children, and teachers leave the sanctuary during the congregational singing of this hymn.

Materials needed

1. red felt for right side of banner, and for boy
2. salmon pink or orange for left side of banner, and for girl
3. black felt or Pellon Phun Phelt for the cross
4. white felt or Pellon Phun Phelt for the letters, chalice, wafer, shell, drops of water
5. black, red, and white felt for the Bible
6. black cord

Note: Since this is a long narrow banner a deep hem gives the banner body; fringe is not necessary.

Use a black felt pen to add a Bible reference to the Bible

14. One True God

Children's Participation

Processional: "Holy God, We Praise Thy Name," TLH, SBH (congregation).
Pastor(s), children, and teachers process into the church during this hymn.

Banners: God the Father, God the Son, God the Holy Spirit

The Choirs: "We All Believe in One True God," *Joyful Sounds,* TLH, TCH
(older children when indicated)

"Thanks Be to God," *Joyful Sounds* (older children after the
benediction)

"God the Father Bless Us," *Sing for Joy* (younger children when
indicated)

The Spoken Word: After the Apostles' Creed is spoken by the congregation,
the children will read what the Bible teaches concerning God the Father, God
the Son, and God the Holy Spirit. Banners indicating each Person of the Trinity
are brought forward as indicated.

1. The Bible teaches that the only true God is the triune God: Father, Son,
and Holy Spirit; not three Gods, but one divine Being. I Corinthians 8:4 states it
clearly, "There is no God but one." Then Matthew 28:19 reminds us of the three
distinct Persons, "Go therefore and make disciples of all nations, baptizing
them in the name of the Father and of the Son and of the Holy Spirit.'

Banner 1: "God the Father" is brought forward.

2. To God the Father we ascribe the work of creation. The Bible teaches
this: Genesis 1:1: "In the beginning God created the heavens and the earth."
Psalm 19:1 also says, "The heavens are telling the glory of God; and the
firmament proclaims His handiwork."
3. Other Bible verses which tell us that God is the Creator of all things are:
Hebrews 3:4: "Every house is built by someone, but the builder of all things is
God," and Colossians 1:16: "In Him all things were created, in heaven and on
earth, visible and invisible."

Older children rise and sing "We All Believe in One True God," st. 1.
Banner 2: "God the Son" is brought forward.

4. To God the Son, Jesus, we ascribe the work of redemption, or salvation.
The Bible clearly teaches this in John 1:29: "Behold the Lamb of God, who
takes away the sin of the world!"
5. Another Bible verse to remember is 1 Peter 2:24: "Christ Himself bore
our sins in His body on the tree, that we might die to sin and live to
righteousness. By His wounds you have been healed."
6. Two more important Bible verses to remember are: 1 Timothy 1:15:
"The saying is sure and worthy of full acceptance, that Christ Jesus came into
the world to save sinners," and Matthew 18:11: "The Son of Man came to seek
and to save the lost."

Older children rise and sing "We All Believe in One True God," st. 2.
Banner 3: "God the Holy Spirit" is now brought forward.

7. To God the Holy Spirit we ascribe the work of sanctification, which means bringing people to faith and keeping them in the faith. 1 Corinthians 12:3 states, "No one can say 'Jesus is Lord' except by the Holy Spirit." 1 Peter 1:5 tells that we "are kept by the power of God through faith unto salvation" (KJV).

Older children rise and sing "We All Believe in One True God," st. 3.

8. We have shown from the Bible that God is triune. We cannot understand this mystery, but we believe it because the Bible teaches it. We thank God for life itself, our faith, and salvation. These gifts are given to us by the triune God.

"God the Father Bless Us" is now sung by the younger children.

Recessional: "Glory Be to God the Father," TLH, SBH. The banners remain in place, and the pastor(s), children, and teachers leave the sanctuary.

GOD the FATHER

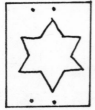  

CREATOR

GOD the SON

 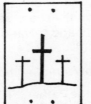 

SAVIOR

GOD the HOLY SPIRIT

COMFORTER

Materials needed

1. two or three shades of green poster board
2. white and black construction paper for symbol cutouts
3. two other colors of construction paper for letters such as light blue, yellow-orange, or light gold
4. heavy green yarns to tie sections of banners together

15. The Holy Trinity: Father, Son, and Holy Spirit

Children's Participation

Processional: "Holy, Holy, Holy, Lord God Almighty," TLH, SBH (congregation). Poster bearer leads pastor(s), children, and teachers into the sanctuary during this hymn.

Poster: Blessed Trinity

The Choirs: "Glory Be to God on High," *Folk Encounter* (younger children)
"Praise God from Whom All Blessings Flow," *Folk Encounter* (older children)

The Spoken Word: Children will explain the doctrine of the Holy Trinity, and they will read from the *Concordia Bible Story Book* about the baptism of Jesus.

1. Who is the only true God? The only true God is the triune God: Father, Son, and Holy Spirit, three distinct Persons in one divine Being or Essence.

2. The Bible teaches that there are not three Gods, but one God, and that each person is the full God. Triune means three in one. Human reason cannot grasp the mystery of the Holy Trinity, but we believe it because the Bible teaches it.

3. One of the best Bible accounts to show the teaching of the Trinity is the baptism of Jesus. We will tell you that story now.

4. Jesus came to be baptized because His heavenly Father had commanded Baptism. Besides, in order to be the Savior of the world, He had to keep this commandment as well as all the rest. This is why He said to John, "Let it be done My way; for it is right to do all that the Law requires."

5. Then John stepped with Jesus into the Jordan and baptized Him. As soon as the Baptism was over, Jesus came out of the water praying.

6. Then a wonderful thing happened. The heavens opened, and the Spirit of God came down in the form of a dove and lighted on Jesus. At the same time a voice from heaven said, "This is My beloved Son, with whom I am well pleased."

7. It was the voice of the heavenly Father. He was pleased with His Son because He willingly offered Himself to do all that was needed to be done to save everyone from the everlasting punishment of sin.

8. The universal creeds—The Apostles', Nicene, and Athanasian—are all careful to explain the Trinity by treating each Person of the Trinity, Father, Son, and Holy Spirit, in separate articles. The creeds were necessary to clearly set forth the main teachings of the Bible. As we confess our faith next in the words of the Apostles' Creed, let us think about the Trinity.

The Silent Prayer: Children will sing the common doxology, "Praise God, From Whom All Blessings Flow."

The Recessional: "Glory Be to God the Father," TLH, SBH (congregation). Poster bearer, pastor(s), children, and teachers leave the sanctuary during this hymn.

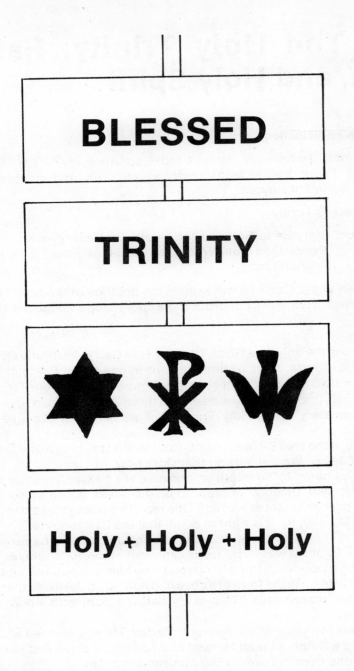

BLESSED

TRINITY

Holy + Holy + Holy

Materials needed

1. bright green poster boards for sections 1, 2, and 4
2. light green poster board for section 3
3. white construction paper for letters
4. black construction paper for silhouette symbols and crosses

68

16. Pray for Peace Between Nations

Children's Participation

The Processional Hymn: "Before the Lord We Bow," TLH, SBH (congregation). The national flag, the Christian flag, and the banner lead the procession with pastor(s), children, and teachers following. Immediately after the hymn is finished and all the children are in place, they will face the national flag, place their hands over their hearts, and give the pledge of allegiance:

I pledge allegiance to the flag of the United States of America and to the Republic for which it stands, one nation under God, indivisible, with liberty and justice for all.

Children and teachers face the Christian flag and pledge to the cross:

I pledge allegiance to the cross of the Lord Jesus Christ, and to the faith for which it stands, one Savior eternal, with mercy and grace for all. So help me, God.

Banner: Pray for Peace

The Choirs: "God Bless Our Native Land," *Joyful Sounds,* TLH, SBH, TCH
"Beautiful Savior," st. 4, *Joyful Sounds,* TLH, SBH, TCH (after the benediction)

The Spoken Word: Responsive reading of Psalm 47, TEV, by pastor, children, and the congregation. A bulletin insert will have been prepared.

PASTOR: God goes up to His throne! There are shouts of joy and the blasts of trumpets, as the Lord goes up!

CHILDREN: Sing praise to God; sing praise to our King!

PASTOR: God sits on His sacred throne: He rules over the nations.

CONGREGATION: The rulers of the nations assemble with the people of the God of Abraham.

PASTOR: More powerful than all armies is He; He rules over all!

ALL: Sing praise to God; sing praise to our King! God is King over all the world; praise Him with songs!

As part of the prayers for the day, the following litany for peace will be read with the pastor, children, and congregation. (This can also appear in the bulletin insert.)

PASTOR: Almighty God, our heavenly Father, Ruler of the nations, we pray for the President, Vice-President, Congress, and all others who are in authority in our country.

CHILDREN: Teach them to walk in Your ways and govern our country according to Your will.

PASTOR: We pray also for the leaders of *all* nations.

CONGREGATION: Teach them to walk in Your ways and govern their countries according to Your will.

PASTOR: Give to all leaders good health and protect them from harm and danger.

CHILDREN: Teach them to walk in Your ways and to govern their countries according to Your will.

PASTOR: Give the leaders of all nations courage to work together, to serve the needs of the people; and Lord, bless their efforts so we may have peace among all nations.

CONGREGATION: Teach them to walk in Your ways and to govern their countries according to Your will.

ALL: We pray in the name of Jesus Christ, whom You sent to be our Savior, the Savior of all people and nations. Amen.

Recessional: "All Hail the Power of Jesus' Name!" TLH, SBH. The national flag, Christian flag, and banner lead the group. Pastor(s), children, and teachers come to the center aisle and leave the sanctuary while singing.

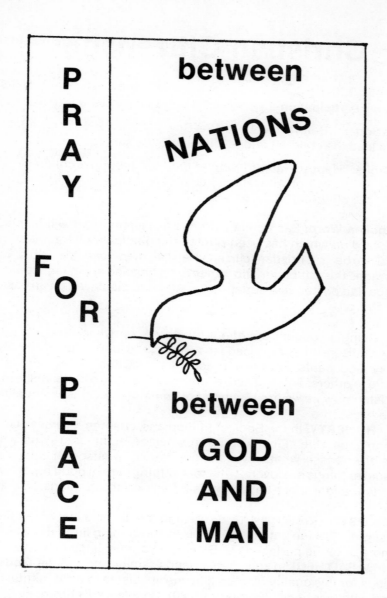

Materials needed

1. background—two colors of felt such as light blue for the left side and avocado green for the right side
2. Pray for Peace—black felt
3. other letters—light blue, or light yellow-green
4. dove—white
5. olive branch—light green
6. fringe and cord—white

Note: Other combinations of blues and greens are pretty, such as yellow-green for the left side, royal or medium blue for the right side.

17. Christian Citizenship

Children's Participation

Processional: "Before the Lord We Bow," TLH, SBH (congregation). The pastors lead the children and teachers into the sanctuary.

The Choirs: "Happy, Happy," *Sing to the Lord* (younger children)
"Lord of All Nations, Grant Me Grace," *Joyful Sounds,* (older children)

The Spoken Word: Each child who has a speaking part will display a large visible card on which has been printed the quality or characteristic which is needed to be a Christian citizen. He will then read the Bible verse that encourages this characteristic. When he is finished speaking, he will tack the card or a flag poster on a burlap-covered board displayed on an easel in front of the church.

1. Being a good citizen of our country is a privilege and a blessing from God. As citizens of our blessed land we have responsibilities and should live the way God wants us to live, practicing our Christian way of life to be an example to others. This will help to make our country a better place in which to live. Listen now as we are reminded of some of the Christian qualities we all should have.

2. **HONESTY.** In the Book of Philippians, chapter 4, verse 8, God tells us to live an honest life. "Finally brethren, whatsoever things are true, whatsoever things are *honest,* whatsoever things are just, whatsoever things are pure, whatsoever things are lovely, whatsoever things are of good report; if there be any virtue, and if there be any praise, think on these things." Be an *honest* citizen.

3. **JUST.** In Proverbs 4:18 we are told that living a just or fair life is like a bright light. "But the path of the just is as the shining light, that shineth more and more unto the perfect day." Be *just* in your dealings as a citizen.

4. Be **FAITHFUL** to your work, friends, family, and spouse. God promises blessings for this quality of good citizenship. Listen to it: "A faithful man shall abound with blessings" (Proverbs 28:20). Be a *faithful* citizen.

5. The Good News Bible says a **RELIABLE** person is really refreshing. This is the Bible verse: "A reliable messenger is refreshing to the one who sends him, like cold water in the heat of harvesttime" (Proverbs 25:13). Be a *reliable* citizen.

6. Be **KIND.** A kind person enjoys a happy life. Kindness is a virtue every Christian citizen will want to cultivate. The Bible says, "Be kind and tenderhearted to one another, and forgive one another, as God has forgiven you through Christ" (Ephesians 4:32 TEV). Be a *kind* citizen.

7. **LOVE.** Love God and your neighbor; then our country will be a better place in which to live. The Bible says this about *love*: "This is what love is: it is not that we have loved God, but that He loved us and sent His Son to be the means by which our sins are forgiven. Dear friends, if this is how God loved us, then we should love one another" (1 John 4:10-11 TEV). Be *loving* citizens.

8. **COURAGE.** It takes courage to be a Christian. In Deuteronomy 31:6 God tells us to have courage, for He will be with us: "Be strong and of good courage, do not fear or be in dread of them: for it is the Lord your God who

goes with you; He will not fail you or forsake you." A Christian citizen needs *courage*.

9. **BLESSED.** If we practice these Christian virtues and keep God first in our lives, and if all people in our country do this, our nation will be truly blessed. This is what the Bible says about a nation being blessed: "Blessed is the nation whose God is the Lord; and the people whom He hath chosen for His own inheritance" (Psalm 33:12 KJV). Be *blessed* citizens.

Recessional hymn: "To Thee, Our God, We Fly," TLH. Pastor(s), children, and teachers leave the sanctuary during the singing of this hymn.

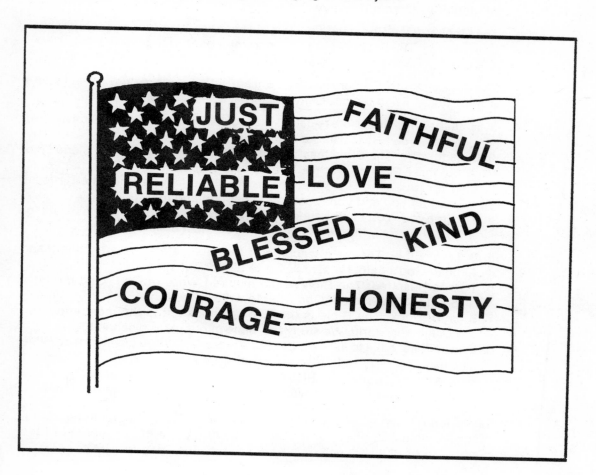

Materials needed

1. one large display board, about 3'x4'; light blue, light green, or white
2. one large flag poster made out of construction paper or fadeless art paper, about 24"x36"
3. construction paper for cards for the 8 words
4. 2" letter patterns and construction paper for letters

18. The Bible Shows Us the Way to Heaven

Children's Participation

Processional: "God's Word Is Our Great Heritage," TLH, SBH (congregation). Pastor(s), children, and teachers process into the sanctuary during the singing of this hymn. The hymn may have to be sung twice.

The Choirs: "One Book and One Way," *Primaries Sing* (younger children)
"The Word of God," *Sing to the Lord* (younger children)
"How Precious Is the Book Divine," *Joyful Sounds* (older children)

The Spoken Word: Primary children will add letter cards to cutout placed on a display board when they present the acrostic, HOLY BIBLE.

1. **H** is for holy. The Bible is called the Holy Bible because it is God's Word. God is holy. He is without sin.
2. **O** is for one. The Bible teaches that there is one God. There is one God, but three Persons, Father, Son and Holy Spirit.
3. **L** is for love. The Bible teaches us that God loves all people. He loves you and you and you (pointing to people) and me.
4. **Y** is for you. You must believe the Bible. No one can believe in Jesus for you. You are important to God and you must believe in Him.
5. **B** is for Bible. The main teaching of the Bible is that we are sinners and need God's help. He sent Jesus to die for our sins.
6. **I** is for inspired. The Bible is the inspired Word of God. God the Holy Spirit told the men of God what to write in the Bible.
7. **B** is for book. The Bible is the Book of books. It is the most important book in the world. We study the Bible in our church schools.
8. **L** is for like. I like to listen to the Bible lessons. Do you like to attend Bible class? Do you like to read your Bible? I do.
9. **E** is for everyone. The Bible is for everyone. It has Good News for everyone. We pray that everyone will believe the Bible and live by it.

Recessional: "Almighty God, Thy Word Is Cast," TLH, SBH (congregation). Pastor(s), children, and teachers leave sanctuary during the singing of the hymn.

Materials needed

1. one large display board, about 3' high—light gold, light green, or beige
2. large black Bible cutout, about 20"x26"—construction or fadeless art paper is good
3. nine black cards, 3½"x5"
4. white construction paper, and 3" letter patterns

19. The Importance of Christian Training

Children's Participation

Processional Hymn: "By Grace I'm Saved, Grace Free and Boundless," TLH. Two poster bearers will lead pastor(s), children, and teachers into the sanctuary.

Posters: The Lord of Love Has Come to Us
You Spread His Love to Everyone

The Choirs: "When We Walk with the Lord," *Joyful Sounds* (all children)
"Pass It On," *Folk Encounter* (during offering, older children)

The Spoken Word: Children read the account of Timothy's early Christian training as found in the *Concordia Bible Story Book,* "The Call to Macedonia."

1. "When Paul and Silas came to the city of Lystra, they met a young man named Timothy. During his early childhood, his mother, whose name was Eunice, and his grandmother, whose name was Lois, had taught him the Old Testament Scriptures.

2. "In this way Timothy learned about the creation of the world, about Adam and Eve, and the fall into sin; also about such great men of God as Noah, Abraham, Moses, Samuel, and David. Most important of all, Timothy learned the prophecies that told of the coming of God's Son into the world to save all people from sin.

3. "And so it was that through the Scriptures the Holy Spirit led Timothy to faith in the God of Israel. And now years later, when Paul preached that Jesus was the Messiah whose coming the prophets had foretold, Eunice, Lois, and Timothy became believers in Christ Jesus as the Savior from sin. This made them Christian believers.

4. "The people of the little congregation in Lystra spoke highly of Timothy. They praised him for his humility and for his understanding of the Word of God.

5. "Paul was so pleased with Timothy that he wanted to take him along on his missionary trips as a helper and a friend. Timothy was willing to go.

6. "Soon he was on the way with Paul and Silas, traveling from congregation to congregation and preaching to the people. The result was that the believers were strengthened in their faith and new believers were added to the church every day."

7. We must take our Christian training seriously. We need to make use of the opportunities our church provides for Bible study and worship. Then we, like Timothy, will grow strong in our faith. We do not know how God may use us in His kingdom.

Recessional: "My Hope Is Built on Nothing Less," TLH, SBH. Poster bearers, pastor(s), children, and teachers leave the sanctuary during the congregational singing of this hymn.

Materials needed
1. light gold poster boards
2. black construction paper for Bible, cross
3. bright red construction paper for heart, Bible pages
4. white letters for Holy Bible
5. red and black letters for captions

20. The Luther Seal

Children's Participation

Processional Hymn: "A Mighty Fortress Is Our God," TLH, SBH (congregation). The banner bearer will lead the pastor(s), children, and teachers into the sanctuary.

Banner: Live by Faith in Jesus

The Choirs: "Beautiful Savior," TLH, SBH, TCH, *Joyful Sounds* (during the presentation, by the younger children)
"Happiness Is the Lord" *Folk Encounter, Folk Hymnal* (older children)
"Onward, Christian Soldiers," TLH, SBH, TCH *Joyful Sounds*

The Spoken Word: With the use of an overlay (transparency) of Luther's seal projected to a screen with an overhead projector, children explain the meaning of the seal. If an overhead projector and transparency are not available, make a large seal out of felt and attach to a display board.

Part I

1. When Martin Luther read in the Bible that the Lord Jesus is the one and only Savior for all people, he began to tell everyone about Jesus and His great love.

2. He told the story of man's salvation by translating the Bible into German, the language of his people. He also wrote the catechism, a book used to study the main teachings of the Bible.

3. He preached many sermons and taught many classes from God's Word. He also wrote many hymns and taught people to sing them. One of his greatest hymns is "A Mighty Fortress Is Our God," which we sang this morning.

4. There was another way that Luther told the story of salvation to others. In his day it was always the custom of royalty and all great families to have a crest, or family coat of arms, which appeared on all their belongings. These were usually symbols of important events in their lives, or it would depict some great quality the family had.

5. Luther prepared such a coat of arms, or emblem, which told the news that meant so much to him: salvation through faith in Jesus. It is sometimes called the Luther rose because it is the picture of a flower. This Luther emblem has become a "coat of arms" for the Lutheran Church and is also called Luther's seal. This is what it looks like and what it means:
Overlay 1 is projected showing the black cross.

6. In the center of the emblem is the black cross. Black is the color of mourning that reminds us of our sins. It was on the cross of Calvary that Jesus died to save people from their sins. It was God who loved the people of the world so much that He gave His only Son; everyone who believes in Him will not perish, but have eternal life.

Overlay 2 is projected showing the red heart.

7. The cross is planted in a red heart. The heart is a symbol for our own hearts. It reminds us of the blood of Jesus Christ, which makes us clean from

every sin. We believe in our hearts that Jesus is our Savior, and we are put right with God.

Overlay 3 is projected showing the white rose.

8. The red heart is centered in a white rose. The white rose is a symbol for Jesus. The Bible calls Jesus the rose of Sharon. White stands for purity or holiness and also reminds us of light. Jesus said He is the Light of the world; and we, his children, find comfort, joy, and peace in Him. He is our beautiful Savior.

Children sing: "Beautiful Savior"

Part II

Overlay 4 is projected showing the blue field.

9. The white rose is set in a blue field. Blue is the symbol of heaven and the color of hope. When we trust in Jesus as our Savior, we know that in all things God works for our good because we love Him. We have real joy in knowing that we have His help here on earth, and that we have life with Jesus in heaven.

Overlay 5 is projected showing the gold ring, and the seal is now complete.

10. The gold ring that encircles the Luther rose is the symbol of eternity and the color reminds us the hope of heaven is precious. The joy of heaven will never end, and our salvation in Jesus is a most valuable gift.

Completed seal remains projected

11. And so we have the Lutheran emblem—a Christian coat of arms —composed of the black cross, the red heart, the white rose, the blue field, and the golden circle. This symbol of our faith is a Christian badge of honor, a reminder that the children of God should live by faith in Jesus Christ our Lord.

Children sing: "Happiness Is the Lord"

The Recessional: "Onward, Christian Soldiers." Children sing st. 1, congregation sings sts. 2—4 while pastors, children, and teachers are led out of the sanctuary by the banner bearer.

LIVE BY FAITH IN JESUS

Materials needed

1. background—gold burlap
2. letters and cruciform—black felt
3. cross—red
4. fringe, cord—white
5. lamb, banner—white felt

21. How God Used His Servant Martin Luther

Children's Participation

Processional Hymn: "A Mighty Fortress Is Our God," TLH, SBH.

Display: The Just Shall Live By Faith

The Choirs: "The Bible Is a Wonderful Book," *Sing to the Lord* (younger children)

"God Is Good, We Come Before Him," *Children Sing 2* (older children)

The Spoken Word: Children will tell how Martin Luther translated the Bible from Hebrew and Greek into the German language, thus placing God's Word into the hands of the common people. He also wrote the Large and Small Catechisms to aid in the instruction of children.

1. Martin Luther, servant of God, translated the Bible into the German language, wrote two catechisms, and wrote many other volumes on Bible teachings. It happened like this. On April 26, 1521, Luther was leaving the city of Worms, Germany, bound for his family home of Moehra. He left Moehra in the early part of May for Wittenberg. As he and his companions were riding along at dusk, a group of armed men rushed out of the forest and captured him, placed him on a horse, and hurried off into the forest.

2. The news of Luther's capture spread from village to village. All the people heard was that he had been taken by the enemy. Many believed that he was killed and mourned his death. The enemies rejoiced and thought they were now rid of Martin Luther, the man who dared to speak out against the sinful practices in the church.

3. God was with Luther, and had more work for him to do. Luther's captors were not enemies, but friends. They had followed the orders of Elector Frederick and taken Luther to safety secretly. Luther was to remain in hiding because his very life was in danger.

4. Luther's friends took him to a castle. They arrived at about midnight and the heavy drawbridge of the Wartburg Castle was slowly lowered. They entered the castle, and here is where Luther remained for a long time.

5. Luther disguised himself as a knight. He let his beard grow, carried a sword, and was called Junker Georg. On occasion he would go with the other knights of the castle to go hunting, but he did not find much pleasure in this. While here he was still able to carry on correspondence with friends at Wittenberg. Messages were sent by courier, but Luther would not tell even his friends where he was. He referred to his hiding place as the "region of birds."

6. The work that God led Luther to do here was to translate the Bible into the German language. The German versions of the Bible were crude, inaccurate, and not readily available to the common people. Luther realized he would have plenty of time to translate the Bible while in seclusion at the Wartburg. So he began this great work.

7. This work required much time and patience. Luther said that a translator must know how the mother in the home, the child in the street, and the common man in the marketplace express themselves. Therefore he mixed

in with the people at the marketplace to get a feel for the way in which they expressed themselves.

8. Great care was taken in making sure the translation was accurate. We are told that he would inquire from many people for the exact German name of animals, reptiles, and birds mentioned in the Bible. Sometimes it took several days to decide upon a correct word to use. His work was blessed by God, for his translation became the most widely used in Germany.

9. It is hard to believe that Luther finished translating the New Testament in less than three months. In 1522 the New Testament of the Bible was in German print. He did not begin translating the Old Testament at the Wartburg Castle. The entire Bible was not finished until 1534. After this, revisions and improvements were made on the translation. Luther's great work inspired others to translate the Bible into the English language and others.

10. Luther loved children. He looked upon their instruction in the Word of God as being very important. He urged parents to give their children Christian instruction and training. To help them, Luther had schools organized throughout Germany, making certain that instruction in the Bible and Christian training were an important part. He wanted the schools to be truly Christian.

11. The benefits of the Reformation for us and the world are many. Besides making the Bible available in the language of the people, and stressing the importance of education and liberty, the main teaching of the Bible was once again restored.

12. The most important teaching of the Bible is the Gospel message. Salvation, given by God thorugh faith in Christ Jesus, was the real message of the Reformation. All other teachings in the Bible depend on this important doctrine.

13. We thank God for His servant Martin Luther, who was not afraid to bring back to the people the important message that faith in Jesus is the only way to receive salvation. Good works do not earn our salvation, but are a fruit of our faith in Christ.

14. The important question is, What can we do now? As God's people we must make sure that the Gospel message of the Bible continues to be taught in our churches and schools. We can all be involved in Bible study in our churches, schools, and homes. It is urgent that we are regular in our church attendance and support of God's work. We want to be faithful followers of our Lord and Savior, Jesus.

Recessional: "Lord, Help Us Ever to Retain," TLH, or "For All the Saints," TLH, SBH. Pastors, children, and teachers leave the sanctuary during the singing of this hymn.

The just shall

live by faith.

Rom. 1:17

Materials needed

1. one large display board, light gold background
2. one large open Bible cutout, about 24"x36", construction paper or fadeless art paper
3. letter patterns (about 2"—2½") and black construction paper
4. glue for the letters
5. cutouts of a German Bible and catechism to add to the display

22. Praise And Thanksgiving

Children's Participation

Processional: "We Praise Thee, O God, Our Redeemer, Creator," TLH, SBH (congregation). The banner bearer will lead the pastor(s), children, and teachers into the house of worship. Before being seated, the children approach the Communion rail or steps leading to the altar and place their gifts of canned goods, which will be given to needy families. Note: the sanctuary may be decorated beforehand with autumn colors, with apples, pumpkins, squash, gourds, and other local produce.

Banner: May the People Praise You, God

The Choirs: "Thank You," *Folk Hymnal for the Now Generation* (older children)
"We Thank You, God," *A Child's Garden of Song* (younger children)
"Thank You (Litany)," *Children Sing, Book 2* (older children) (after the benediction older children encircle the congregation and sing this selection)

The Spoken Word: Psalm 67, TEV, is read responsively by the pastor (or DCE or teacher) and the children.

PASTOR: God be merciful to us and bless us.
CHILDREN: Look on us with kindness.

PASTOR: That the whole world may know Your will.
CHILDREN: That all nations may know Your salvation.

PASTOR: May the peoples praise You God;
CHILDREN: May all the peoples praise You!

PASTOR: May the nations be glad and sing for joy,
CHILDREN: Because You judge the peoples with justice and guide every nation on earth.

PASTOR: May the peoples praise you, God;
CHILDREN: May all the peoples praise You!

PASTOR: The land has produced its harvest;
CHILDREN: God, our God, has blessed us.

PASTOR: God has blessed us;
CHILDREN: May all people everywhere honor Him.

The Prayers: Just before the General Prayer five children will approach the microphone and read the Thanksgiving prayers they have written under the teacher's or pastor's guidance. The pastor may announce that five children will lead us in prayer. Topics for prayers should include:
(1) parents, home, and family; (2) church, school, pastors and teachers; (3) our nation and its leaders; (4) Jesus, forgiveness, and salvation; (5) life itself and the opportunity to live for God.

Recessional: "Praise to the Lord, the Almighty," TLH, SBH. Banner bearer, pastor(s), children, and teachers leave the sanctuary.

Materials needed

1. background—brown burlap
2. cutouts—four colors of Pellon Phun Phelt such as yellow, yellow-orange, orange, yellow-green, gold, or aqua
3. letters—white or light beige felt
4. black felt pen to put details on the cutouts before glueing them on the banner

23. Prophecies of the Messiah

Children's Participation

Processional Hymn: "Comfort, Comfort Ye My People," TLH, SBH (congregation). One banner bearer will lead the pastor(s), children, and teachers into the sanctuary. Children reading prophecies will carry their stars.

Banner: Rejoice! Emmanuel

The Choirs: "Oh, Come, Oh, Come, Emmanuel," TLH, TCH, *Joyful Sounds* (older children)
"Mary, Mary," *Hymns Hot and Carols Cool* (younger children)
"Jesus, Our Good Friend," *The Little Christian's Songbook* (youngest children)

The Spoken Word: "The Prophecy Tree." In place of the Old Testament lesson the children will share assigned prophecies of the Messiah. Each child will place a star—with the prophecy reference on it—on the prophecy tree, which has been made in the form of a lighted Christmas tree. As they place the star over a socket, they turn the bulb on, thus lighting the star.

Introduction: (Narrator) Throughout the Old Testament God promised to send the Messiah. Each prophecy shed more light on who this Messiah would be and what the Christ would do for all people. We want to share some of these prophecies with you today, from the *Good News Bible: the Bible in Today's English Version*. As each light is turned on the prophecy tree, may the true identity of the Christ Child give you much joy.

1. The very first promise of the Messiah was given in the Garden of Eden, to Adam and Eve. This prophecy is recorded in Genesis 3:15, where God spoke to the serpent: "I will put enmity between you and the woman, and between your seed and her seed; He shall bruise your head, and you shall bruise His heel." *(Child now places the star on the prophecy tree and turns on the light).*

2. Speaking of Abraham's descendants, from whom the Savior would come, God said: "His descendants will become a great and mighty nation, and through him I will bless all the nations" (Genesis 18:18). *(Place your star on the tree.)*

3. When Jacob called for his sons, to tell them what would happen in the future, he gave another Messianic prophecy—"Judah will hold the royal scepter, and his descendants will always rule. Nations will bring Him tribute and bow in obedience before Him" (Genesis 49:10). *(Place your star on the prophecy tree.)*

4. In Numbers 24:17 Balaam uttered this prophecy of Jesus' coming. "I look into the future, and I see the nation of Israel. A King, like a bright star, will arise in that nation. Like a comet He will come from Israel."

5. This next prophecy reminds us that Jesus would come from King David's descendants. "The royal line of David is like a tree that has been cut down; but just as new branches sprout from a stump, so a new King will arise from among David's descendants. The Spirit of the Lord will give Him wisdom and the knowledge and skill to rule His people. He will know the Lord's will and will have reverence for Him" (Isaiah 11:1-2).

6. The prophet Isaiah, in speaking with King Ahaz, gave this prophecy of

Jesus: "Well then, the Lord Himself will give you a sign: a young woman who is pregnant will have a Son and will name Him 'Immanuel' " (Isaiah 7:14).

7. Another prophecy in the Book of Isaiah is familiar to all Christians. This prophecy is found in Isaiah 9:6. "A Child is born to us! A Son is given to us! And He will be our Ruler. He will be called 'Wonderful Counselor,' 'Mighty God,' 'Eternal Father,' 'Prince of Peace.' "

8. It was even prophesied that Jesus would be born in Bethlehem, as the next prophecy from Micah 5:2 tells us. "The Lord says, 'Bethlehem Ephrathah, you are one of the smallest towns in Judah, but out of you will I bring a Ruler for Israel, whose family goes back to ancient times.' "

9. Concerning the work of the Messiah, Isaiah 40:3 speaks of John the Baptist, who would prepare the way for the Lord's coming. This is the prophecy: "A voice cries out, 'Prepare in the wilderness a road for the Lord! Clear the way in the desert for our God!' "

10. In the New Testament Jesus referred to Himself as the Good Shepherd. This relationship was prophesied many years before in Isaiah 40:11: "He will take care of His flock like a shepherd; He will gather the lambs together and carry them in His arms; He will gently lead their mothers."

11. The triumphal entry of Jesus into Jerusalem on the first Palm Sunday, of Holy Week, was prophesied in Zechariah 9:9. "Rejoice, rejoice, people of Zion! Shout for joy, you people of Jerusalem! Look, your King is coming to you! He comes triumphant and victorious, but humble and riding on a donkey—on a colt, the foal of a donkey."

12. When Jesus died on the cross for us, He was forsaken by God. This was prophesied in Psalm 22:1. "My God, My God, why have You abandoned Me? I have cried desperately for help, but still it does not come." Jesus was truly left alone to suffer for all people.

13. Jesus' suffering was prophesied by Isaiah. "We despised Him and rejected Him; He endured suffering and pain. No one would even look at Him—we ignored Him as if He were nothing" (53:3).

14. The next prophecy continues to tell us that Jesus endured our suffering for us. "But He endured the suffering that should have been ours, the pain that we should have borne. All the while we thought that His suffering was punishment sent by God" (Isaiah 53:4).

15. Verse 5 of this same chapter makes it clear that Jesus took all this punishment for our sins. "But because of our sins He was wounded, beaten because of the evil we did. We are healed by the punishment He suffered, made whole by the blows He received."

Conclusion: (Narrator) The people of the Old Testament waited and longed for the coming of Jesus, the Messiah. When He came, many did not receive Him as their Lord. During Advent, we too, wait for the Lord of Christmas. Will you receive Him as your Lord and Savior?

Recessional: "Lift Up Your heads, Ye Mighty Gates," TLH, SBH (congregation). Banner bearer, pastor(s), children, and teachers leave the sanctuary during the singing of this hymn.

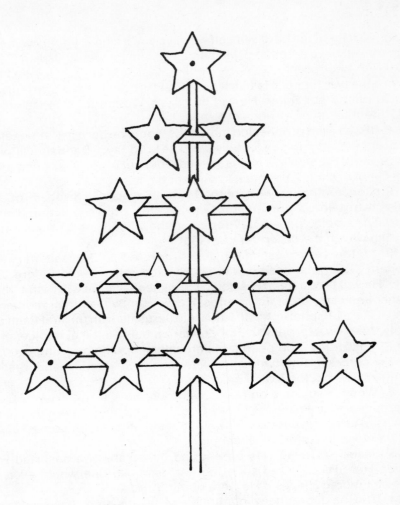

Materials needed

1. white poster board to make stars
2. outdoor lights (all white) or large indoor lights
3. masking tape, staples, hammer to attach light cords
4. green paint for the tree

Note: This service is especially beautiful in the evening, during the Advent season.

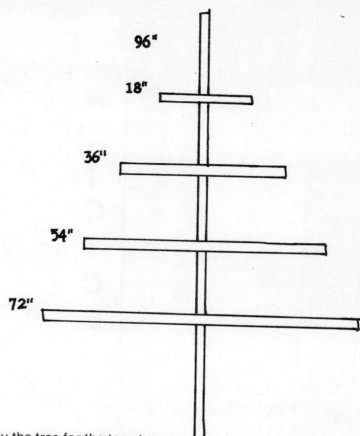

Materials needed

The prophecy tree
1. 1"x2" boards, nailed back to back
2. screws to attach cross bars
3. fifteen 17" stars

Note: You may need to have a child steady the tree for the top stars.

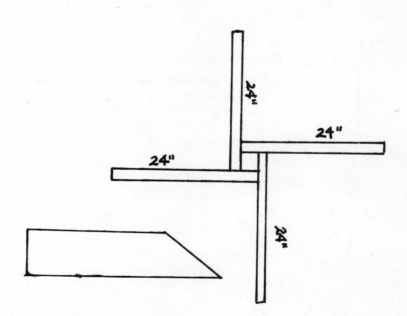

The stand
1. 2"x4" boards (8')
2. nails

This tree will probably be too big for space available in some churches. The center pole could then be 7' and the bottom cross bar 5'. Stars should be 13" then. Plan your own scale.

89

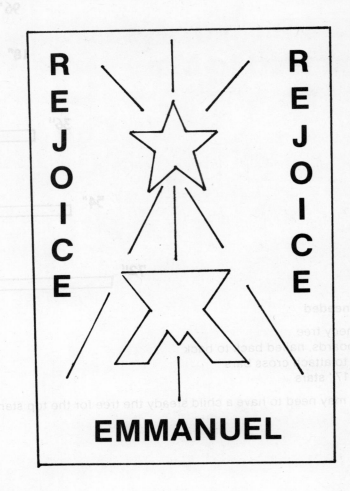

Materials needed

1. background—bright red or red-orange or magenta felt or burlap
2. manger—black felt
3. star—yellow felt; light beams, light yellow
4. Emmanuel—white felt
5. Rejoice—black felt

24. The Birth of Jesus Announced to Mary

Children's Participation

Processional Hymn: "O Lord, How Shall I Meet Thee," TLH

The Choirs: "The Magnificat," TLH, TCH. (The older children sing while the pantomime motion choir performs in the front of the sanctuary. Motions are included in this service. Choose eight girls from the junior high age for the motion choir.)
"Every Year the Christ Child," *Joyful Sounds* (younger children)

The Spoken Word: Selected children will read the account, "Mary and the Angel," taken from the *Concordia Bible Story Book.*

1. Beautifully situated among the hills of southern Galilee was a quiet little city of a few thousand people called Nazareth. In one of the humble homes of Nazareth there lived a God-fearing young woman whose name was Mary. She was engaged to be married to a carpenter named Joseph. Mary and Joseph were poor, but both were descendants of David, the great king of Israel.

2. One day about six months after the angel Gabriel had appeared to Zechariah, the same angel appeared to Mary in her home. God had sent the angel to bring her some wonderful news. "Greetings, most favored one!" the angel said. "The Lord is with you!"

3. Greatly disturbed, Mary wondered what this greeting might mean. The angel explained it, saying, "Do not be afraid, Mary, for God has been gracious to you. You see, the Savior is to be born, and God has chosen you to be His mother. You shall name Him Jesus. He will be great, and He will be called the Son of the Most High God. The Lord will give Him the throne of His forefather David, and He will rule as King in the hearts of His people forever."

4. What an honor for Mary! Through one of His angels God Himself had told her that she would be the mother of His Son Jesus, the promised Savior of the world; therefore Mary believed that the message was true.

5. But she was puzzled. An ordinary young woman like herself, engaged to be married but not yet living with her husband, would be the mother of God's Son? Most strange!

6. "How can this be?" Mary asked the angel. The angel told her that what seemed impossible God would make possible. By the power of the Holy Spirit she would become a mother; therefore the Child that would be born of her would be the holy Son of God.

7. To strengthen Mary in her faith that God could keep His promise to her, the angel said, "Elizabeth, your relative, although she is very old, will also have a son. Every promise of God is sure to be fulfilled."

8. After Mary had heard this, she said, "I am the servant of the Lord. May all things happen as you have said." Then the angel left her.

9. The news Mary had received was too wonderful to keep to herself. Quickly she got ready and hurried to the place where Zechariah and Elizabeth lived. Elizabeth knew, for the Holy Spirit had told her so, that Mary would be the mother of Jesus the Savior.

10. As soon as Mary greeted her, she said, "You are the most blessed of all

women. And blessed is the Child that God will give to you. But why do I have the honor of having the mother of my Lord come to me? How blessed you are because you believed the word of the Lord! He will make all He told you come true."

11. Mary was so happy that from deep in her soul there came the words of a beautiful hymn of praise. "My heart is overflowing with praise for the Lord," she said, "and my soul rejoices in God my Savior, for He has looked with favor on me, His lowly servant. From this time forward all believers will call me blessed, because He who is mighty has done great things for me. Holy is His name! Because He is merciful, He has helped the people of Israel, as He promised to Abraham and to His descendants forever."

12. After visiting with Elizabeth about three months, Mary returned to her home. When Joseph learned that Mary would become a mother, he was troubled. But being a godly man, he did not want to disgrace Mary; so he decided to set aside their marriage agreement in a private way.

13. But this was not pleasing to God. To change Joseph's mind, God had an angel appear to him in a dream and say, "Joseph, do not fear to take Mary home as your wife. By the Holy Spirit she will have a Child. She will give birth to a Son, and you shall name Him Jesus, for He will save His people from their sins."

14. All this happened to fulfill the prophecy the Lord made through the prophet Isaiah when he said, "The virgin will be with Child and give birth to a Son. He will be called Immanuel." This name means "God with us."

15. After the angel had spoken to Joseph, he was satisfied. In keeping with the will of God, he took Mary to his home as his wife.

(Older children now sing the Magnificat, and the Pantomime Choir performs)

Recessional: "Hosanna to the Living Lord," TLH, SBH. Pastor(s), children, and teachers leave the sanctuary during the singing of this hymn.

The Magnificat with Motions for Pantomime Choir

(From "Christ Is Born Today," a children's Christmas Service, CPH, 1968)

Girls from the junior high age should be robed in white and perform the motions as indicated. Children will sing the Magnificat while the girls perform.

My soul[1] doth magnify[2] the Lord: and my spirit[3] hath rejoiced in God,[4] my Savior. For He hath regarded the low estate[5] of His handmaiden: For, behold, from henceforth: all generations shall call me blessed. For He that is mighty[6] hath done to me great things: and holy[7] is His name. And His mercy[8] is on them that fear Him from generation[9] to generation. He hath showed strength[10] with His arm. He hath scattered[11] the proud in the imagination of their hearts. He hath put down[12] the mighty from their seats: and exalted[13] them of low degree. He hath filled[14] the hungry with good things: and the rich He hath sent[15] empty away. He hath holpen[16] His servant Israel in remembrance of His mercy: as He spake to our fathers, to Abraham, and to his seed forever. Glory[17] be to the Father, and to the Son, and to the Holy Ghost; As it was in the beginning, is now, and ever shall be: world without end. Amen.[18]

1. Arms are crossed on chest.
2. Arms are extended straight and upward at a 45-degree angle.
3. Arms are crossed on chest.
4. Arms are extended straight and upward at a 45-degree angle.
5. Kneel with head bowed and hands folded at middle of waist.
6. Extend right arm straight and upward at a 45-degree angle (kneeling).
7. Arms are extended straight and upward at a 45-degree angle (kneeling).
8. Hold hands straight up over head and bring them down slowly to simulate the coming dawn of mercy (kneeling).
9. Stand facing partner. Extend hands straight and toward one another.
10. Extend right arm straight and upward at a 45-degree angle (kneeling).
11. Twirl around once and end facing chancel wall.
12. Kneel suddenly with head bowed.
13. Stand up and face audience.
14. Go to center and all place hands together. (Two groups may be needed)
15. Step quickly back to positions.
16. Form semicircle—or two semicircles—and face towards the chancel cross.
17. Standing in position No. 16, extend arms straight and upward at a 45-degree angle.
18. Turn around, face audience, drop hands.